BEAGLE TALES 7

By

BOB FORD

SUNBURY PRESS

Mechanicsburg, PA USA

Published by Sunbury Press, Inc.
Mechanicsburg, Pennsylvania

www.sunburypress.com

For information about special discounts for bulk purchases, please contact Sunbury Press Orders Dept. at (855) 338-8359 or orders@sunburypress.com.

To request one of our authors for speaking engagements or book signings, please contact Sunbury Press Publicity Dept. at publicity@sunburypress.com.

ISBN: 978-1-62006-900-4 (Trade Paperback)

Library of Congress Control Number: 2018959191

FIRST SUNBURY PRESS EDITION: September 2018

Product of the United States of America
0 1 1 2 3 5 8 13 21 34 55

Set in Bookman Old Style
Designed by Crystal Devine
Cover by Lawrence Knorr
Cover Photo by Bob Ford
Edited by Lawrence Knorr

Continue the Enlightenment!

Pushing the Limit

Labor Day is upon us, marking the unofficial end to summer. Sure, the Astronomers have their mid-September date, but the meteorological summer ends as we leave August. Here in Pennsylvania, it marks the beginning of dove season. If you are like me, then you flush a lot of birds while your dog is chasing rabbits. I happened to be having a friendly conversation with a game warden when I asked him, "Say, would it be legal to hunt doves with a beagle?"

"What?" he looked at me in disbelief.

"Well," I said, "My beagles are constantly bumping doves into the air while they are looking for rabbits or chasing them."

"Oh," he said, "Well you can shoot birds with your rabbit dog in rabbit season."

"Yeah, but could I let the dog chase rabbits before rabbit opens, and only shoot doves that might be flushed."

"That would be dog training while carrying a long gun. That is not legal."

"But," I held my index finger in the air to make a point, "What if I was bird hunting the whole time and my dogs just happen to be prone to running off game—rabbits."

"Ha!" he laughed, "I don't think that is going to work."

"Yeah, I figured that would be pushing the law. But, I seriously wouldn't shoot any rabbits."

"I know, but it isn't going to look that way."

If I am honest, I am always looking for a new or creative angle to do things. And I am not talking about pushing the letter of the law, though I was in that particular instance. I am old enough to remember when Labor Day was not a day devoted to laboring, which it seems to be now. There was a time when people were off work, often with pay. Now, people go to work for the holiday, and they may even have two jobs.

1

Dad and I would usually run dogs the Sunday before, while mom and Gram got things ready for the big cookout. For the most part, at our house, our cookout had a lot of salads that were not really salads. I think of a salad as a bunch of vegetables, with lettuce being the main ingredient (though I prefer spinach). Our family cookouts featured potato salad, macaroni salad, bean salad, and pasta salad. I realize that macaroni is also pasta, but as near as I can tell, the featured ingredients in pasta salad were pepperoni, salami, and cheese. Of course, there was Jell-O salad for dessert. This was made of Jell-O), fruit, and whipped cream. Basically, I am saying that none of the salads were heavy in leafy greens. Naturally, we also had a wide array of meat ranging from hot dogs to hamburgers, to bratwurst, and usually steak.

"Load up the dogs," Dad told me one Sunday evening before Labor Day. Steam poured into the living room from the kitchen. This was before air-conditioning was commonplace, and all of the boiling water was making the house uncomfortable. Sometimes, September is more like August. But it took a lot of elbow macaroni, rigatoni, and potatoes to create all of those non-salads. Mom made two types of potato salad—the cold kind, and a hot potato salad with a vinegar dressing. All the boiling started Sunday, so they could be made and cooled in the fridge. Some of those salads contained mayonnaise, and it had to be kept cool. As memory serves me, there was always a lively debate between mom and Gram over the use of Miracle Whip and Mayonnaise. My mom preferred the former, her mom preferred the latter. There could often be subterfuge when it came to this ingredient.

"Bobby," Gram would whisper to me, "Distract your mom so I can add mayonnaise before she ruins the whole thing with that miracle whip."

"I'll try," I said, "But I don't really care which one we eat.

"Hush," Gram said, "There is nothing miraculous in that stuff but some sugar and less oil."

Gram lived through The Great Depression when Miracle Whip was cheaper than traditional mayonnaise. It was a

2

stigma to use it. My mom just liked Miracle Whip better.
One time, my Gram dumped out the Miracle Whip from
its container and replaced it with mayonnaise. I wouldn't
say that mom was as mad about the switcharoo so much
as she was about the waste of money. Miracle Whip
and mayonnaise cost about the same money today. The
container was almost full.

"I have to load up the dogs, Gram," I looked at Dad,
who was filling jugs with water for the dogs to drink. Dad
moved from the kitchen as mom poured a pot of boiled
spuds into a strainer that was resting in the sink. The
kitchen windows steamed immediately and I ran out the
door to get the hounds.

"I think we just missed a Miracle Whip fight," I said to
Dad as the old pickup groaned up the hill.

"Timing is everything," Dad said, "And I think that this
truck needs to have the timing adjusted soon."

My whole family is full of guys that can fix cars. They
can tune carburetors (some of them still have cars with
carburetors!) and time an engine by ear as well as most
mechanics do with a timing light. Myself, I have AAA,
which is anathema in my family. My dad never owned a
new vehicle in his entire life. "Used cars are cheaper if you
know how to fix them yourself."

We ran dogs until after dark. Today, that might mean
midnight or two o'clock in the morning. Back then, it
meant that you let them chase until it turned dark. Then
you called them in after they holed the rabbit or lost it. On
that night, it was pretty late when we got them. Probably
ten o'clock. It was a cooperative rabbit and a cool evening,
compared to the daytime temperatures.

"Let's do this tomorrow," I said to Dad, "It is going to
cool off nice".

"And miss the picnic?" he asked, "You think we will get
away with that?"

"Sure. We just leave real early, and be back in time to
eat."

"You know that we have to move the tables around in
the morning to get things ready," he puffed his pipe, "It
isn't going to work."

When we unloaded the pooches into the kennel and walked into the house and into the laundry room, mom and Gram were sitting at the kitchen table.

"Why would we use canned blueberries for this Jell-O salad, when we have frozen blackberries?" Gram asked my mother.

"I told you," Mom said, "I am emptying cabinet space for when the sauerkraut is ready and it will be fine with blueberries."

"This makes no sense to me," Gram sighed, "We have blackberries."

Dad stopped me as I was about to enter the kitchen, "Let's go set those tables up," he said.

"Now you are talking," I quietly clapped my hands and rubbed them together. So, in the dark, by porch light, we set up the tables and chairs.

"You meet me in the kitchen by six o'clock tomorrow morning," Dad said.

"No problem," I nodded my head.

This leaving for the woods with dogs, of course, was always done on Thanksgiving. Dad and I always went rabbit hunting that morning. But that was different, hunting season was limited to a few months per year, and the days that Dad was off work during rabbit season were an even smaller number of days. It was a long-established tradition that he hunted on Thanksgiving. Of course, no one complained about that.

Labor Day? Could we really miss the morning to simply run dogs and not even hunt? We would listen to hound music all the time, it wasn't a rarity or some once-in-awhile treat to be enjoyed like a Thanksgiving hunt provided. We could condition those beagles anytime, and we just did that very thing the night before, picking the dogs up 8 hours before we planned on running them again. On rare instances when we did go a long time in between rabbit chases, our standard excuse was, "Those dogs need run. They are going stir crazy and we don't want them bothering the neighbors by barking at every songbird that lands in the yard." That excuse clearly would not work here. To be honest, the dogs seemed shocked when I went to get them at 5:30 in the morning, before first light.

"Are we really doing this?" was what their eyes seem to say, and they wagged their tails with enthusiasm as they realized we were headed afield. I put them in the old Ford, and we headed into the briars at the beagle club to await the morning, a thermos of coffee on the seat, and a couple fresh donuts stuffed into a brown paper sack and resting on the dashboard. Evidently, Mom and Gram made some donuts the night before.

"Was Mom awake?" I asked.

"Not yet. I left a note on the dresser."

"Oh yeah?"

"Told her that today was Labor Day and all I have ever done was labor. Said I was going to the woods for the morning," He said. A note. I still remember the good old days of notes. No texts, no phones in your pocket. You could go all day without being in contact with anyone. You made all of your phone calls in the evening when people were home.

"You tell her it was my idea? She won't get mad at me," I said.

"No, I left you out of it. Just like I didn't tell her that we are really running dogs so that we don't have to listen to her and her mother debate what spoon to put in a bowl."

"Hah. Yeah. Mom doesn't really care what spoon goes into a bowl until Gram changes things and makes it more complicated. Then she has an opinion!"

"Heh!" Dad chuckled, "Who cares if the spoon has holes in it if you are serving baked beans."

"Gram does," I said and we laughed harder.

This might seem like a small thing—running dogs on Labor Day, but it was a big thing at the time. In all honesty, we were home by nine o'clock in the morning with tired dogs and ready to eat. I hadn't really thought about that note since that morning. Dad certainly did labor. He took every bit of overtime he could get and did extra jobs during the daytime when he was on night shift. He was constantly remodeling kitchens or putting on new roofs for extra income. Labor Day often makes me nostalgic for those times. I have decided to take things to a whole new level of pushing the envelope for this year's holiday.

"Want to go camping for Labor Day weekend," I asked my wife, Renee.

"Campgrounds will be packed!" she said, "That's the last weekend of summer."

"Yeah, I know," I opened the refrigerator, looking for a snack but not knowing what I wanted, "But we could camp someplace and run the dogs on a few rabbits. Leave after church on Sunday, and spend Monday in the briars. We could have a nice cookout. I'll get those marinated pork chops from that one butcher?"

"Ooh," Renee said, "Maybe we could. Wes has to work that day." Wes is her son, my stepson.

"Maybe we can do something with him when he gets out of work on Monday night," I said.

"Good idea," she said, "Can we make side dishes to go with the chops? We can put food in a cooler, right?"

"Yeah," I said, "No worries."

"I'll go get the ingredients," she said, "The last time I sent you to get them you grabbed Miracle Whip instead of Mayonnaise."

I stood stark still and wondered what spoons we might be taking with us.

BEAGLEMANIA

"Did you pick up hamburger buns?" my wife, Renee, asked as I walked in the door with the fourth beagle from the truck. We have a double door system. There is a door between the living room and my wife's craft room. That room opens into the parking lot. The dogs are not allowed in her room. Instead, when I run dogs, they all hop onto the living room couch to happily receive their SportDOG Tek 2.0 collars. They have no idea that the collars track them or can correct them. All they know is that they wear them to chase rabbits. Heck, even if I forget to charge the collars and will not be using them, they wear one. Those collars mean rabbits to them. Then they get carried, one at a time, through my wife's room (door closed behind me) and then to the truck (door closed behind me). This is to prevent hounds from getting into the yard unattended. We live in a residential area, and the rabbits won't usually come near the house, but the churchyard is full of them. I reverse the process when I return home, carrying each into the living room.

"What buns?" I asked.

"The buns we talked about before you left!" she held both arms outward, palms facing up. This is her sign language for "You're an idiot" in case she ever does it to you.

"Well," I said, "If you told me while I was in another room, I probably didn't hear you." She is notorious for talking to me from another room in the house or even another floor. I've killed too many rabbits and missed way too many for my hearing to be able to hear her talking from the kitchen while I am in the basement. Especially since her voice gets higher pitched as it gets louder. She may as well be a dog whistle when she gets really loud.

"No!" I read her lips. She was loud, "I looked you in the eye and told you to bring back hamburger buns for supper when you were done running dogs."

"Really?" I asked.

"Yes," she said, "But you were talking about trying a new spot to get ready for rabbit season."

"Hey," I said, "I did try a new spot today. How did you know?"

"Because," she outstretched her palms facing upwards, "We had a whole conversation about it."

"I don't remember."

"Of course not," she muttered, "You are diseased. Beaglemania."

"What?"

"Beagles take over vast portions of your brain. It is crazy."

"That's not true."

"How long did it take you to find names for the last pups that you kept?

"Why?" I asked.

"They were months old before you found names," the palms went up.

"So?"

"My friend Michele picked a name for a human baby within a week after knowing she was pregnant. In fact," Renee pointed at me, "She picked two names. A boy name and a girl name."

"You know that I make puppies earn a name." I defended myself. They need a name that suits them. Maybe your friend should have done the same."

"You can't take a nameless baby home from the hospital and register it later!" Renee said, as I gently pushed her arms back down.

"I am sorry about the buns. I can go get them now," I said, "I need dog treats anyway,"

"AHA!" I read her lips again. Although she may have said another three-letter word that starts with an A. It was pretty loud. "That's another symptom of beaglemania," she said, "We always have dog treats."

"It helps keep the dogs obedient. Positive reinforcement," I said. I get small treats. And will make

8

them lay "down" or come "here" to get one. Commands I use in the woods.

"Right, but have you ever noticed that you aren't worried about human food being in the house?" Renee asked.

"I do too."

"Remember when I asked you to go out and get ice cream one night and you said it was too late?"

"Yeah," I said.

"What time was it when you went for dog food the other day? It was late."

"Well, I was out of feed."

"No, you had plenty of dog food."

"Sure, the Performance blend of Purina ProPlan. You know I give the Bright Minds mix to the old timers that are mostly retired."

"They couldn't eat a different food one night?" she asked.

"Would you like me to get some ice cream while I am out getting the buns?" I asked. I thought that I was making a peace offering.

"Are you saying that I am heavy?" she looked at me.

"No, why?"

"Well, then why did you offer me ice cream right now?"

"Because I didn't get it when you asked for it the other night," I considered raising my arms in the air, palms up, but decided against it at the last second. She shifted gears.

"Then there is the truck," Renee said, "Another sign of the mania."

"How could this be true?" I asked.

"You own a truck. We literally had to borrow a truck to move a couch into my mother's apartment," she said.

"What's that have to do with anything?" I asked.

"You have the rooftop tent over the bed, the dog box in the bed, and a permanent storage thing that shortens your bed by a couple feet. Then swinging boxes on the bumper that prevent using the truck with the tailgate lowered, because those swinging storage bins have to be closed."

"Yeah, it is a sweet ride. But," I said, "I got the couch moved. And the guy that owned the truck helped me carry it. I couldn't carry it by myself anyway. It was a hide a bed. So, it is good that my truck is only useful for hunting rabbits."

"Can you name a single TV show that they are making?"

"Everybody Loves Raymond," I said.

"Those are all repeats," Renee said.

"Really?"

"Yeah, you aren't tuned in to popular culture at all."

"That's not bad, is it?"

"Do you even know what music Wesley listens to?" Wes is my stepson.

"It has a lot of bass, a distinct lack of melody, and fast lyrics," I said.

"So, do you know the artists?"

"No."

"But could you tell me what dogs are doing well at the trials and what their pedigrees are?"

"I could tell you the dogs doing well," I said, "But I don't study pedigrees. I could probably only give you a generation or two."

"That's part of the beaglemania," Renee said.

"Yeah, you can tell that some of those dogs didn't earn a name. Almost no thought put into some of their names," I said.

"Is that right?" she laughed.

"Yeah, but I get it. Some guys are keeping whole litters, not buying one or two pups. It's tougher to put the time into the name at that point when you are naming 8 of them. Sometimes the dog with the least creative name turns into the best one."

"Least creative?" She asked.

"I am not fond of human names."

"Well, beaglemania is a manageable disease," she said, "As long as you get to run dogs more days per week than you do not. It keeps you pleasant. There are worse things that a guy could be doing than chasing rabbits with beagles."

"That's a good point," I said. I will go get those buns. I walked out to the truck and was contemplating what dog treats to get. The smaller the better, but I always go with what is on sale, and break them into smaller pieces if need be. I determine which one to buy after calculating the cheapest price per ounce (by weight) of treat. I was thinking that perhaps that was part of the beaglemania when Renee called my cell phone, right before I got into the truck.

"Hello?"

"Get some ice cream too. Something with chocolate. And don't get the cheapest hamburger buns. Get the ones made with potato bread." Potato bread, buns, and rolls are common here. They use regular flour mixed with a potato flour as well.

At the store, there was a lot of dog treats to sort through, but I did it. I was almost to the cash register when Renee called again.

"Did you get potato buns?"

"Yes," I answered.

"Did you get the chocolate ice cream?" she asked.

"Of course," I said.

"Okay. Love you. See you soon."

"I love you too," I hung up. And got out of line at the cash register to go get the ice cream.

SKILLS

A couple years ago, I was hunting snowshoe hare in New Hampshire with friends, Kris Ford (no relation) and Jason Wiseman. Wiseman and I were in my truck, and we were following Kris. We stopped along a dirt road when we saw some other guys that were out hunting hare as well.

"Hey guys!" Kris said loudly. He says everything loudly.

"How are you?" one of them said.

"Great!" Kris said, "Jason and Bob are here to hunt," he motioned to us.

"Hello," I shook their hands.

"These guys," Kris said as he pointed at our new friends, "Are here from New York state. They are the Albanians."

"I didn't realize that they refer to people from Albany as Albanians," I said.

"Do they?" Jason said.

"I think so," I answered, these guys are from New York. Albany is in New York."

"We are not from New York," one of the guys said.

"I thought Kris said you were?" I asked.

"They live in New York now," Kris said.

"Do they live in Albany?" I asked. It is the capital of the state, so I figured it was likely.

"No," Kris said, "They are originally from Albania."

"The country?" I asked.

"Yes," the one gentleman laughed. Do you know much about Albania?"

"I know that for some reason they always have Albanians as the bad guys in action movies. That can't be correct."

"It isn't," one laughed, "Or is it?" he looked me in the eye.

"I would think that Hollywood is just being mean," I gulped, "No one that runs beagles can be bad!"

"You're right!" the guy said and we all laughed. Heh. Ha. Whew. Seriously, they were great guys. And I told you this story so that I could share a line from the "Taken" movie where Albanians were bad guys. "I have a very particular skill set," is what the hero of the movie says. Skills are important, and we can't all do everything.

One Sunday, a few months ago, I was planning to take the beagles out for some exercise when I got a phone call from a church member, Wanda.

"Pastor Bob," she said when I answered my cell.

"Yep. What's up?"

"There is water in the electric panel box."

"Surely, there can't be."

"There is. We went to use the stove, and it was plugged in but not working. We opened the breaker box and saw water in there. Dripping."

"Well," I said, "It has been raining a lot. Could it get in there from the meter head?"

"I have no idea, that is why I called you. We decided the power should be turned off. You want to go do it?"

"Sure," I said and we hung up. On my way to the church, I decided to call my hunting buddy, Lee. He's an electrician. He hooks up factories to the grid, so I was sure he could talk me through our little problem. I explained the situation and told him I was supposed to shut the main breaker off to cut power to the church.

"You got rubber boots?" Lee asked.

"Sure," I said, "I run dogs in wet grass all the time. But I am wearing dress shoes now.

"You have rubber gloves?" He asked.

"No."

"Is there water on the floor in front of the breaker box?"

"I have no idea," I answered.

"Best thing for you to do is come get me before you blinking kill yourself." Only, he didn't say blinking. He took care of it for us, rubber boots and gloves and all. I had no idea what I was doing and probably could have zapped myself into the hereafter.

This is how it is in life. We need each other for help with things where we lack "a particular skill set." My wife, Renee, and her friends will often sit around and talk abound husband skills. One time, while we were at a supper that she had to attend for her job at Penn State, the topic arose.

"Does Bob do landscaping?" Jen asked Renee.

"Uh, not really," Renee said and looked at me, "He cuts the grass before it gets so long that the lawnmower can't handle it."

"Oh, so Bob is a homebody. Does he do housework for you?"

"I have him trained pretty well. Now that we have been married all these years."

"Does he clean windows?"

"Well, no." Renee glared at me again, "But he now puts his dirty dishes in the sink, and will often put his dirty clothes in the hamper."

"That is what you call trained?"

"Yep," Renee said, "And it took 13 years."

"I also put the toilet seat down sometimes," I beamed with pride.

"Well," Jen looked at me, "If you aren't a landscaper or a house cleaner, what do you do?"

"I go to the woods. I bring animals home, and put them in the freezer."

"Animals?" Jen squinted her eyes in disdain for the vagueness."

"Deer, turkey, grouse, woodcock, dove, squirrels, pheasant, trout, perch, bluegill, walleye, and rabbits."

"Rabbits?" Jen said, "I was reading about rabbits. Could you teach my husband to shoot rabbits?"

"It's not too hard to do," I said.

"We will just give you some rabbits," Renee said, heading off any possibility that her coworker's suburban hubby would return to his home with a story that might make things awkward for Renee at work."

"You put all that stuff in one freezer?"

"Ha. No," I said, "We have a few freezers."

"I really think," Jen said while biting her lip, "I want Ron to learn how to shoot rabbits. I was in a restaurant in

Monterey while at a work conference, and rabbit was $20. But they told us how healthy it is, and I am interested in getting more."

"Yeah," I said, "The rabbits I get are smaller, and probably not as tender as the cage raised bunnies you ate."

"Interesting," Would you mind if Ronald went with you?"

"Nah. He can go," I said. Renee looked upset.

"You are the first husband I have met that has these talents."

"The talents mostly belong to the dogs. It seems like we buy a lot of ammunition," my wife said, "$20 rabbit sounds like a real deal, to be honest."

As we got into our car after the dinner, my wife turned to me and said, "Don't you dare embarrass me by taking him hunting!"

"Relax, I said, "It is still months until rabbit season."

"I will hope she forgets about it by then," Renee stared out the car window as I started the engine.

I got to thinking about what she said, about the dogs being the real stars of a rabbit hunt. More than that, I was thinking about how I wish all the dogs were superstars (field champions), but they aren't. Sure, they place in trials and win once in a while, but they aren't field champions. In some ways, my pack has specialists with particular skill sets. Granted, they can all find a rabbit and run it to the gun—solo or in a pack—but they each shine at different moments. Badger is my dog that can find rabbits when my others struggle to jump one. Hoss keeps the rabbit pushing ahead and gets many of the small breakdowns. If there is a long check, and the dogs have lost the rabbit for a half minute or more, it is usually Duke that resolves the matter. Blitz and Diamond are tiny—even for 13" class, and they can stand out from the pack in those really thick blowdowns, where the others are on their bellies and still trying to get lower to follow the rabbit.

I ran into Jen the other day, at the grocery store. She was getting artisanal food (whatever that is) and I was buying dog food. I had run out, and the place I usually buy it (Tractor Supply) was closed.

"Hello, Bob!" she said.

"Hi there," I said.

"You don't remember my name, do you?"

"Sorry."

"I'm Jen," she said, "We met at a work thing that your wife and I attended." I have been buying venison. It is more expensive than rabbit.

"I am sure it is."

"Well, you had mentioned venison that evening, and I wasn't sure what it was. It is deer?"

"Yep."

"Well, I have Ron ready to deer hunt!"

"Good," I said, "There are plenty of them."

"Can you take him?"

"Maybe," I said, "I will have to ask the guys that let me hunt with them."

"Okay," Jen winked, "I hope you can work it out. I really like venison. Will your venison taste the same?"

"Oh," I said, "I don't know. I never bought it. But this venison is at least free range."

"Free range is the expensive beef!" she shrieked.

"Oh yeah?"

"It sure is. I bet free-range venison is better too!"

"Good, call Renee before Thanksgiving and we can get your man ready."

I threw the dog food in the back of my truck and went home. Now, we are in September, and hunting season is just around the bend. I have my pack of beagles looking ready for the rabbit season, and I couldn't be happier. I am very ready to leave the heat and humidity of summer behind. In fact, I was out for a rabbit chase on cool morning dew, just yesterday, when my cell phone rang. It was my wife.

"Hello?"

"When did you talk to Jen?"

"Who?"

"The $20 rabbit lady..." Renee described her in terms I would remember.

"Ohhhh," I said, "When I was getting dog food at the grocery store. She was buying deer meat."

"Yeah," Renee laughed, "She is walking around the office talking about free-range venison. What do you have to say for yourself?"

"I have a very particular skill set."

"What?"

"Never mind."

Field Corn

It is August, and that means that we are getting closer to two things that are related, at least for me, here in Pennsylvania. Longer chases and corn. Let me explain. By late August, we will be getting some cooler mornings, hopefully, and that means that the dogs will be running more, in preparation for hunting season. I will probably brace or solo dogs, in my favorite hunting spots, to assess the population of rabbits in each location. A couple of those locations are near farms or at least land that is leased by farmers, and there are chases that start in the brush and then go into a 100-acre cornfield. Sometimes, the chase never leaves that corn, and when it is time to go home I have to wade into the rows of stalks and catch the beagles.

Many of you might live in states that do not allow year-round running in the wild, and it was once that way here in Pennsylvania until good science showed that training dogs does not have much impact on rabbit population at all. Not compared to the crows that will kill an entire nest of babies at once, or the fox and coyotes that kill rabbits with regularity. When I was a kid, we were allowed to return to running dogs in the wild in late August or early September as I recall. For some reason, I think it was late August, and it is because of this story that I am about to tell you.

As kids (teenagers) we would go camping with some regularity. It didn't even require much preparation. We just grabbed a tattered tent and went. None of our tents were "waterproof" so we always set them up under a canopy of trees and put plastic tarps above them, tied to the limbs so that any rainfall would be diverted away from the tents. Naturally, when you pitch a tent under trees, you will have a certain number of roots under your tent floor. No matter how hard you tried to find a spot free of roots, you would have some. As a result, once your tent was set up, you would roll around inside to find a spot that was mostly free of protruding tree roots. Once you discovered the angle you would have to lie down to be comfortable, you would then put your sleeping bag in that exact location. It was not at all uncommon to find yourself along one edge of the tent, or at a 45-degree angle, or curved into a C shape.

In late summer, we always preferred to camp near a large farm. Why? Well, many people may not realize this, but if you cook field corn (the stuff grown for livestock) within an hour or two after picking, it tastes as good as sweet corn. Don't get me wrong, it doesn't taste as good as the best sweet corn you ever ate, but I guarantee it is better than the worst sweet corn that you ever had. It is even better the decent sweet corn that you bought at the grocery store for a lot of money. We started to boil the water before we even picked the corn, and we cooked it within minutes of taking it off the stalk.

We would often go camping on Friday or Saturday night when we did not have work the next day. My friend Steve never had work the next day (he never had a summer job), and he also had a truck of his own, so he would drive.

"Hey," I asked, "Can we haul the beagles out?"

"What?" he asked.

"I wanted to take the dogs to get a chase. I am sure we will get a rabbit up and running by the farm."

"Your old man makes you take care of dogs all week, why do you want to haul them along?" Steve shook his head.

"I haven't been able to run dogs too much lately," I said, "So all I have done with them is shovel poop and feed them. But if you don't want them, just say so."

"No, go ahead," Steve said.

A big part of camping was talking to your friends. I see my own stepson texting his friends with immediate responses, followed by additional texts. We didn't do anything like that. You saw your friends whenever you bumped into them. In school, it had to be when you had a class together. Depending on your schedules, you might only see them once or twice in a given day. In the summer, you would go to common hangouts to see who might be there. Perhaps the ballfield, or maybe the pizza joint. Even the telephone was no guarantee that you could get a hold of someone. First of all, there were no cell phones. Secondly, there was no caller ID or call waiting. You might call somebody 3 times in 3 hours and never get it to ring because the number you were calling was already in use. You would get—a busy signal, something almost unheard of today. This was especially true if you called a house with lots of kids. I had a dozen phone numbers memorized back then, maybe more. I do not know any numbers now, due to cell phones. Anyway, camping was a time when you got to talk. Maybe too much.

"I loaded Duke and Princess into a plastic dog crate that we packed into the bed of Steve's truck with all of the rest of our camping gear, and we headed for the oasis. That was the name we gave this spot because it was a grove of trees that marked the boundaries between several large farms. This was in a more civil time when trees or large rocks would serve as boundaries instead of a wall of posts with yellow signs that said: "PRIVATE PROPERTY DO NOT ENTER." The farmers knew each other and trusted that things would go well. The boundaries were great places to find rabbits because the hedgerows and briars grew there. This was before farmers felt a need to plow every square inch of available land. For the most part, no farmer cared if we camped unless we left a mess. So, we always made sure to clean up after ourselves. I always packed a big garbage bag.

We got there Friday evening, right after we all got off work and Steve picked us up, one by one, in his pickup. I rode in the bed of the truck, making sure that the plastic dog crate didn't slide around. That would have been difficult, given all the gear we packed. You'd swear we were looking for The Northwest Passage and packed twice the equipment necessary to get there. As soon as we arrived at the oasis, I turned the dogs loose and started pitching my tent. Steve had a dome tent, which was relatively new then, and expensive. It set up fast. The rest of us had cheaper models with lines and pegs and stakes and every

other kind of contraption you could imagine. You had
to retighten ropes once in a while. Mine was purchased
from Sears. Remember Sears? My family would drive 9
miles to a Sears, which had a handful of appliances in the
store and a catalog. The appliances would sell, whenever
someone had a refrigerator or hot water tank quit working.
Everything else was ordered through the catalog, and in a
week, you would drive 9 miles again to go pick it up. I now
own a camping hammock instead of a tent. I ordered it
online, it came to my house two days later.

At any rate, I could set up my Sear's tent in about 10
minutes, which was a blistering speed then. To be fair, I
used it a lot and that helped. I might need 11 minutes on
the first camping trip of the summer. My tent was soon
ready, and I could hear the beagles were in a cornfield.
Some people say that cornfields are tough chasing. Very
often it is hard packed dirt in between the rows of stalks.
My dogs seemed to be doing well, and I let them run while
I started a fire. We put potatoes in aluminum foil and laid
them at the edge of the fire. I grabbed a pillowcase and
headed into the cornfields before dark, so I could get the
choicest of the field corn. I looked for the ears that were
ready, but not so ripe that they might be starchy. The
beagles came within 20 yards of me, though I didn't see the
rabbit. I must have spooked it though, because it squatted
and after a long breakdown Princess nosed it into a sight
chase and the dogs slalomed through the corn, moving
away from me.

By the time I returned to the campfire, the guys had a
pile of wood gathered and were examining the meat.

"What do we have tonight?" I asked.

"We got steaks!" Kevin said. He often raided his family
freezer for these trips, and his family would get a whole or
half cow every year."

"Nice!" Steve yelled.

"They should be about thawed by the time the potatoes
are cooked. I took them out of the freezer right after work,"
Kevin set them near the fire.

I set the sack of corn down, and we placed the large
kettle over the coals. We always had a big fire, but our

stone fire ring had a little protrusion or "keyhole" where we could put a grate for cooking. As the larger fire burned down into coals, we would push those coals under the grate with a shovel or a stick. Usually, it was a stick since we almost always forgot to bring a shovel. Then we added more wood to the larger fire—for ambiance.

"Spuds are done!" John said, and he rolled them a few feet from the fire—into the keep warm setting. I shucked the corn and dropped it into the boiling water. Once the corn was in the water, Kevin put the steaks on the grate, the same grate that held the big pot of water. It was dark, and we were about to feast like kings.

"That rabbit hasn't come out of there, has it?" John asked.

"Nope," I said, "It might not either. I am sure there is a groundhog hole or two in there too."

We ate in silence since we were all hungry. I set some of my steak—there was enough that we could all have two steaks or some people three—aside for the dogs. I would mix it with their dog food later. School was around the corner. So, four guys did what they are prone to do.

"So," Steve said, "I think Susan is looking better than ever."

"Better than Jane?" John asked.

"I like Amy," Kevin said. "How about you Ford?"

"I like 'em all!" I said and we had a big laugh.

I saw the rabbit. Well, I saw its eyes as it poked out of the cornfield. Then it was gone. The dogs emerged, ran along the edge of the corn, and then back into the maze of maize.

"I am glad that we raided Kevin's freezer," Steve said, after watching the beagles, "Because Ford always brings rabbit from his house." That generated another belly laugh from everyone, including me. There were some nights, in late August, on the Allegheny Plateau region of Pennsylvania, when you would cover tomato plants to protect them from a frost in late August. I am not saying it happened every year, but I certainly remember taking the same plastic tarps that we used for camping and trying to put the tomatoes underneath, using tall wooden stakes in the middle to keep the tarp off the plants. It has been years since we had an

August frost. On this night, it was cold enough for a long sleeve shirt, if you were not close to the fire. I decided to not wear an extra shirt, but the cool air on my back let me decide that the dogs were not going to overheat.

We talked about girls for a long time. Then we argued over the best truck manufacturer. When we had exhausted that topic, we moved on to .30-06 vs. .308 for a deer rifle. Then it reached a late hour and we just listened to those two dogs, hammering away in that cornfield. Suddenly, I was alone with my thoughts. That was often the case when I ran dogs. I would think about life and where it was going. What would I do with my life? Before long, guys started turning in to bed. John and I were the last two awake, feeding the fire feverishly.

"Graduation before we know it," John said.

"Yeah, I got two years left," I said, "What are you going to do?"

"I'm not sure."

"Me neither," I said.

None of us in that cornfield had parents that had ever gone to college. There were a few hardscrabble stories for each of us. All the while I just listened to those dogs.

"You'll probably go to college," John said, "You have really good grades."

"I dunno," I said, "I guess. If I can get the loans."

"What did you think of supper?" John asked.

"Not as good as when you bring the steaks." We laughed. John lived with his siblings and his mom. Money was tight. All of the steaks in his freezer were venison, no matter what time of year.

"Makes ya wonder what God is doing," I blurted out, and was surprised to hear it. I thought about God, the nature of life, why we live, and all sorts of things whenever I listened to the beagles chase rabbits. And they were cranking in that cornfield.

"Sometimes," John said, "I think God is looking the other way."

"I wonder about that too," I said. The dogs went silent. Soon they walked to the campfire, exhausted, and I gave them water and tied them to a tree to cool down.

"You putting them in your tent?" John asked.

"Hah," I said. "Yeah, after I feed them. In about an hour. But they will also be in the crate. Last time they were in the tent they peed in there." We chuckled again. My beagles were outside dogs then. We talked about our future, or worries, and our hopes. I fed the dogs, and we called it a night.

I reconnected with John a few years ago. It was at Steve's funeral. In the meantime, he had lost a brother and a sister. We have talked a few times since, but I am really thinking we need to do it again, even if we live far apart now. Looking back now, I think I knew I would be a pastor, even then. The hound music has always sent my mind to a place of reflection and wonder. I still wonder about John's thought that perhaps God is looking the other way. I've decided that God has not turned away but sent us to be His presence, in any and all circumstances. I think I need to call John and see if he wants to go rabbit hunting in a couple months, at some of my old hunting spots. I don't know his number, but it is stored in my cell phone somewhere. I have eaten king crab in Alaska, lobster in Maine, chili in Texas, and tacos in California. None of them compare to field corn at the oasis.

Community Garden

As August moves along we will be approaching the end of the hot temperatures (hopefully), the beginning of the school year, and the end of garden season. The school year marches on and I remember full well what it was like to dread the return to classes, the revocation of summer parole, the reunification with the rogue's gallery of characters that inhabit any high school—the popular kids, the bullies, the nerds (that was me), the athletes, and any other group of person that you could label. It really does go that way. We start to assign people a role in life, and then we judge them accordingly.

Way back in the 1900s, when I went to elementary school, high school, college, and seminary; the schools were still labeling kids as early as first grade. Some were viewed as smarter than others—at that early age. By high school, they branched us out into different tracks. Some went business, others vocational. I went academic, and then, of course, there was general.

Here is the thing, they made decisions about us then, and what they felt we could amount to in this world. Today, of course, they have gone in the opposite direction, and we now tell kids that they can be anything at all. The kid picked last in gym class can be a professional athlete, and the guy that could not master arithmetic is told that he can be an astronaut if that is what he wants to do. One thing is for certain, we have not stopped judging people based upon what they do for a living. It is the first question we get when we meet someone new. "What do you do for a living?"

My mother never worked when I was a kid. Well, what I mean is that she worked all day long but never got a paycheck of her own. She was a house mom. A kid at church asked me not too long ago "What does your mom do?"

"Well," I said, "She isn't alive anymore, but until my dad died, my mom was a house mom."

"What does that mean?"

"She did most of the work in the house, and she also looked after my sister and me and made sure we got to the places that we were supposed to be."

"My mom does that too, but she also works at the store."

"That's great," I said.

"My dad thinks my mom should get a better job."

And that is it, isn't it? Some jobs are viewed as better than others. I promised myself a long time ago that I would never judge somebody based on a job. All through college, there were people that thought it was odd that my dad worked in a factory. Not many, since I did go to a state school, but more than you would think. I hung around other guys who were also first-generation college students. To be honest, many of the most disagreeable and spiteful people I know have what the world would call a "good job." By contrast, some of my best friends have jobs that might be viewed as "bad" or "low paying." That all starts young in life. This brings me to another aspect of August, the end of the garden—and the two themes do reconnect.

I will be honest with you; I do not get real excited about gardens. Sure, I plant one, but it isn't because I love the feel of the soil, or like neat rows of carrots. I mostly just want to save some money. I was cured of any romantic notions about gardens by my father, who planted a large one every year, and then made sure that it looked perfect. He mostly did that by making me weed and water the darn thing.

As an adult, I always adopted a different method—planting clover in between the rows of plants and let that clover choke out the weeds. Sure, the clover can get a few inches high, but it holds moisture and you till it into the soil at the end of the growing season to add nitrogen. I like it. It attracts rabbits, but I can live with that, they eat the clover and mostly leave the other stuff alone. Mostly.

Anyway, my wife and I are both pastors, and we could not serve congregations that are any more different. She pastors in State College, home of Penn State University, and I serve in the next county to the west. My sheep are gardeners, like my family and others in rural Pennsylvania. There is a whole August season to "put up" the produce from the garden by canning it and putting it on shelves, or by fermenting cabbage in massive crocks and making gallons of sauerkraut, or by freezing corn that has been freshly cut from the cob, cooked, and then put under cold water before being strained and frozen.

The church next to the house in State College has adopted a "community garden" for the past two or three years now. It feels like it has been a decade. It is a garden, but in reality, it is more like hobbyists. You pay $35 per year and you get to use a plot of land that is ten feet by ten feet, or as my dad would call that, a small group of tomatoes. They frown upon any pesticides and forbid you to use any pesticides if the neighboring plot of ten feet by ten feet has been declared organic. Naturally, most of the plots have been declared organic, so much so that no pesticides are permitted. I am not saying that I spray bug killer everywhere, but I am not a fan of Japanese beetles, and those things are all over the garden. There is a walkway between each plot and a small fence surrounds the whole thing. The gate faces my enclosed yard.

My wife still has a plot there, and it seems ironic to me that at one time I would plant a large garden in the same area. You also cannot have weeds in your garden and can't allow anything to flower that isn't a vegetable, so my clover is on the banned list as well. While the garden was intended to boost the community and feed the masses, it is kind of a cul-de-sac, suburbanite, white-collar, yuppie commune. And by commune, I mean that they all live in town, and just have decided that they do not want to bother tilling the ground in their own yard, and instead pay the $35 for a 10' x 10' plot. Many are new to gardening, but they have read books. I encounter the "garden gang" in the morning and the evening. Typically, it is when I am coming home from letting the beagles chase bunnies.

I often will return from the woods at 8 o'clock in the morning, put the beagles in the house, and then run a hoe between my wife's plants so as to prevent the weeds from getting started. Then I leave for the workday. Keep in mind, the garden isn't 20 yards away from where I park. The first time I helped out with the weeds last year, there was a guy sitting in the middle of his 10 x 10 plot.

"Are you okay?" I asked.

"Yes, why?" he said and straightened his broad-brimmed hat with his hands. He was wearing surgical gloves.

"Well, you've been sitting out here since I got home. Allergic to something?" I pointed at his gloves.

"No," he said while picking a Japanese beetle from the underside of a plant and putting it into a glass canning jar with holes poked into the lid.

"Hey," I said, "That looks like the same thing we used to catch lightning bugs when I was a kid."

"What?"

"You're jar," I said, "We used to catch lightning bugs in a glass jar and pretend it was a lantern."

"Oh," he said, "I never really saw lightning bugs when I was a kid. I know what they are though. Out here in the country, they are everywhere." As he said "country" I could hear the Jake-brakes from a truck on the interstate echoing to my ears.

"We are in the burbs," I said, "But the country isn't far."

"Good," he said, "Because I want to take these beetles there," he held up the jar."

"Pardon me?"

"I've removed them from all of my plants."

"Well," I paused wondering what to say, "But you know that all these other 10 by 10 plots have beetles, right? You will get new ones. And if you picked them all, they will still come back."

"I will be back tomorrow. And clean my plants again. What would you do?"

"I'll tell ya what I used to do, I would use carbaryl on the plants once in a while when the beetles were thick." I found it interesting that the community garden involved tending your own plants and ignoring the others.

"What is carbaryl?

"You probably know the brand name, Sevin."

"The insecticide?"

"Yeah. I kill bugs. Sorry." I was thankful the community garden was always over by rabbit season, or the guy might really be put in an ethical bind when he saw me come home. I have conversations like this with the gardeners all the time. They always see me with beagles. I usually leave the house with beagles every morning. Sometimes I return with the dogs before going to work. If the weather isn't too hot, there are times when the dogs will ride in the dog box all day and they might get a short run in the evening too. Each day varies. Am I going East to Hershey Hospital? Am I going west to hospitals in Pittsburgh? Maybe I am staying close for visits to nursing homes and could possibly take a pooch to see an old timer that used to hunt with dogs.

Here is where the garden really causes me trouble. There is always somebody there. They come before work and after work. If I let the dogs into my yard at six o'clock in the morning, someone is out there. I am usually gone by six, but not when it is too hot to run the dogs. Although they are not supposed to garden after dark, they do. I let dogs out into the yard at 11 p.m. and the gardeners are there. Barking ensues. I spend all summer disciplining dogs for being dogs. They bark at the people just outside the fence and still on "our property." Granted, the church owns the house and yard.

One summer night, I got home in the evening with the dogs and walked into the garden to get a yellow squash or two to cook on the grill.

"Hey," another gardener said as he wiped the sweat from his brow, "You live in the house there with Rev. Renee?"

"Yep," I said, "I sure do."

"I see you here off and on," he said.

"Yeah," that sounds right." I should note that the church where I work has a parsonage as well. I am there some nights, depending on meetings and Bible studies. The dogs tend to travel with me, from one place to the other. This gardener didn't know that.

"Well," he said, "What do you do?" And here we are, back to the way that we decide things about people, strictly on occupation.

"What do you mean?" I asked.

"Well," he said, "What is your job? For instance, I am a staff employee at Penn State."

"That's awesome," I said.

"So, what do you do?"

"Well, what do you see me do?"

"You seem to be gone all day with dogs. Some days you come back. Some days you do not."

"You nailed it!" I said. I didn't feel a need to tell him about funerals, hospital visits, meetings, and Bible studies that happen in between those times when I leave and return. It was then, that I thought of a line I had used on another guy that asked me the same question. "Yes sir," I said, "I am what they call a trophy husband."

The community garden ends this month, and I am ready for it. I would like to mention, for any youngsters reading, that I have enough diplomas to wallpaper a small closet. One of my deer hunting buddies is an electrician, and he makes more money when he is laid off and collecting unemployment than I do when I am working. I am not complaining about that; I knew what life I was called to live when I decided to be a pastor. I am just saying that you should not believe all the hype when you are told what you can be and what you cannot, and how some skills are viewed as more valuable than others. When I see you, I will talk about dogs, or faith, or the weather, or anything. If someone identifies himself with his job, you will find out soon enough. They won't be able to resist telling you. Speaking of that, I have to get going. Renee is yelling at me because the word on the street is that she married a "trophy husband."

Ice Cream

It was pretty commonplace, when I was a teenager, to drive around town all night and see other people in their vehicles and be seen in your own. I, of course, did not have my own car, but my dad would sometimes let me borrow his truck. He always had a truck, but by the time I was old enough to drive he owned a two-wheel drive Ford pickup truck. It was a dozen years old and the Pennsylvania winters had been hard on the body. Luckily, my adult half-brothers were pretty handy with automotive work, and they always managed to keep the rust from showing and the carburetor purring. Carburetors are rare now, and the guys that can fix them are rarer. I still remember that every once in a while, Dad would tear the air cleaner off the truck and pour a small container of kerosene right into the carb and let it roar. He would have me sit behind the wheel and give it some gas so that the smoke roared and the whole thing was burned clean.

Of course, it would carbon up like it did because my dad never drove further than a couple of miles to work in one direction or a few miles in the opposite direction to run dogs. For weeks at a time, the massive V8 engine would never go over 45 miles per hour. August was always the last great rush to "hang out" before school started at the end of the month. In those days, it was not uncommon for a kid to have $500 car with a $600 stereo.

"Wanna go cruising tonight?" you would ask someone.

"I can't!" he might yell, "My car won't start. Must be something in the fuel system."

"How do you know that?"

"Can't be electrical. Stereo still sounds great. Man, that amplifier under the front seat is pretty powerful." Guys would spend hours installing speakers under the back seat and concealing the wires.

It is different now. "Have you noticed kids driving with earphones while they listen to music?" I asked my friend, Bill last week.

"What?" He said. Bill had a really good stereo in his car.

"Have you seen kids wearing headphone while they drive?" I said a little louder, and with some sign language to demonstrate 'headphones' (held my hands to my ears) and 'drive' (I turned) an imaginary steering wheel.

"Yeah, I have," Bill said.

"That can't be safe," I said, "They can't hear."

"You think we could hear with the stereo systems in our cars?"

"Well," I said, "Probably not, but it was loud enough to give a warning to any other motorist that might be in the area!"

My father's truck had no stereo. What color was it? Primer grey. Every once in a while, it got a new coat of primer. There was never a top coat of paint, simply because it was going to go into the woods for firewood, or hunting, or fishing. We never even thought about a briar or branch scraping across the vehicle. That sort of thing happened regularly. So, my dad's truck was ugly. It had no radio. But it always ran. It always started.

"Ford," Bill said, "Can you get your dad's truck to cruise this week."

"Maybe," I said, "I work till three o'clock. He works three to eleven all week. So, I can try to talk him into getting a ride to work from Mom, and then I will have to pick him up at eleven."

"How you going to get him to agree to that?"

"I will tell him that I want to run dogs in the evening for a while it is cooler. Say, from seven until nine."

"We need to be in town before nine, especially if you have to leave at eleven to go get him."

"Alright," I said, but I still have to run the dogs some. I can't leave the dogs at home.

"Fine."

Much to my surprise, Dad went for the idea, and he let me drive his truck to my job. On Monday, I loaded up the dogs to go to the beagle club after work. I put them in the plastic dog crates that were in the bed of the old Ford. There was a locking cap over the bed, with side windows that you could crank open to get air flow into the dogs. I only let them chase 45 minutes before picking up the guys.

"Hey," Jim said, "Let's go to Bob and Mary's Ice Cream."

"That girl doesn't work there every night!" Bill said.

"Even if she does," I said, "She smiles at everybody. Get over it."

So, we headed out of town for ice cream, and I took the primer grey beast over 45 miles per hour for the first time in months. The engine roared to life like it had been waiting for a moment like this. Back then, there were bias ply tires. The old truck had 10 ply tires. One time, two were flat and we didn't even know it until we started loading it full with firewood. It was a lot of rubber. At 55 miles per hour, the road noise from the tires sounded like a freight train.

"YOU KNOW WHAT?" Bill yelled.

"WHAT?" I yelled back.

"IT DOESN'T REALLY MATTER THAT THIS THING HAS NO STEREO."

"I THOUGHT YOU LIKED A STEREO?"

"NOT EVEN MY AMP IS LOUD ENOUGH TO HEAR MUSIC IN THIS THING!"

Bob and Mary's Ice Cream was popular, and people drove for miles to get there. Teenagers are always surprised when I say that you could drive around all night on $5 back then. So, what you would do is find a place in the parking lot, get your ice cream, and then act cool. How would you act cool? Well, you could always lean nonchalantly against the door of your vehicle. That worked well. It also was possible that you would back into a parking spot, leave your windows down, and then play music in order to get other people to flock to your vehicle.

"Ford," Jim said, "Pull in and we can sit on your tailgate." This was a classic attempt at being cool. You sat on the tailgate and you were visible to everyone.

"We gotta lift that cap door up though!" Jim said.

"Why?"

"Cuz of that dorky screen with the beagle chasing the rabbit!"

"When I was 13, I bought this screen that was specifically designed to keep the sun out of your truck bed. There was a painted design of beagles chasing a rabbit. I ordered it from a catalog and gave it to my dad for Father's Day. It had been there ever since.

"That's why we are sitting on the tailgate," Jim explained, "So, that we can lift that cap door and not have that screen be seen."

"You don't think the scratched primer paint will offset the advantage of hiding the cap door?" Bill said, sarcastically. We ordered ice cream and sat on the tailgate.

"What's that noise?" Jim grumbled and looked into the truck bed.

"It's the beagles," I said.

"You brought beagles?"

"Well, yeah, I only got the truck because I told my dad I wanted to run the dogs."

"That's just great!" Jim sighed. Apparently, it was had to act cool with dogs. After a little while, the parking lot was getting full. It wasn't a huge lot, and while some kids would hang out, the older adults would get their ice cream and leave. This was back in the 1980s, so we were smart enough to know that if the lot became too full for new customers, anybody just hanging out should leave and make room.

"I knew we should have brought my Mustang!" Jim said.

"I thought it didn't start?" I asked.

"I'm working on it," he muttered.

"We gotta go soon," I said. We can go to Tastee Freez and get a burger if you want."

"Those darn dogs are still whimpering," Jim said.

"Yeah, they smell food. I am going to let them pee before we go too." I leashed them.

As I started walking the two beagles on a leash in the grass at the edge of the parking lot next to where I parked, all kinds of girls rushed over. Having beagles may not have been cool, but it was cute.

"That was great guys!" Jim said, "Let's go to the Tastee Freez. I will pay for burgers if Ford lets me walk one of the dogs on a leash while we are there.

"Sounds good to me," I said. And for four nights it worked like that. I ran dogs, we drove out of town for ice cream, I dropped the guys off at their house, then I picked Dad up from work. By Friday, the Mustang was fixed and Jim wasn't interested in my Dad's truck.

"Hey, can we meet at Bob and Mary's?" Jim asked. "I'll walk one of your dogs if you want."

"Sure. No problem."

"How's the dog running going," Dad said when I picked him up that night."

"Good," I said.

"Where you been running the dogs at?"

"Club."

"What club?"

"Our club."

"I see."

"Why? I asked.

"Oh, I noticed you put almost 500 miles on the truck this week. That's all."

"Oh," my mouth hung open.

"I raised four sons before you," he patted me on the back, "I'm just glad you didn't lie to me about actually running the dogs." He laughed and slapped his leg as I steered the primer grey Ford for home.

"Well, we might have driven around a little bit after I ran dogs," I said

"I'd say a several hundred miles' worth of a little bit." He laughed.

The August air heated up as we moved closer to the school year. I stopped running the dogs and everything became focused on new school clothes and school supplies. I did manage to get a date the next week. She wasn't from my school district, but she like the dogs. Remember how I told you that old truck didn't have a radio? It didn't have an air conditioner either. It was still sweltering hot as we went for supper, so the windows were down, the 10 ply tires roared on the pavement, and the whooshing wind blew her hair everywhere. I don't mean it looked glamorous in a breeze. It looked like a TV reporter standing outside to tell us what the hurricane is like. She would turn her head towards me to talk and Charlie Brown's teacher made more sense than the words she yelled into the ruckus. Her sentences were garbled in the rushing wind and roar of the road, as her hair whipped against her face. We had a polite supper and a nice ride home. She never called back. That's August and youth.

GRILLING

Every November, the local and national news shows tell us how to cook a turkey as if preparing a Thanksgiving turkey has never been done before, or that it is as complicated as preparing the pufferfish. The pufferfish can cause paralysis or death if cooked improperly. In my opinion, there is no phrase that is used more overused then "This begs the question." That being said, this begs the question, who watched their friends and family eat pufferfish and die, then said, "Well, maybe we just have to cook it different," and then caught another one? No, it is a turkey, and it isn't the most complicated thing in the world to cook.

We are now in the throes of summer, and they are teaching us how to grill like it is some mysterious art. People have been eating food cooked over an open fire since the stone age, and yet we act like it is some secret skill akin to alchemy. The experts on TV talk about "crosshatch grill marks, and resting the meat as if we have never cooked a burger before. Personally, I cook outside all the time, and there is always a cheap propane grill in my truck. In July, I have to run dogs early, due to the heat. I usually cut them loose around four o'clock in the morning, and run until six or seven. This means that I am getting up in the middle of the night, and by the time I pick up the dogs, I am ready for breakfast. What do I like to cook?

Well, I often bring a thermos of coffee with me, but I also keep instant coffee in the truck in case I do not wake up early enough to brew a pot. I know what you are thinking, instant coffee is kinda dreadful. It's a lot better than it used to be, actually, and you don't have to be bothered by the hassle of cleaning coffee grounds from a percolating pot or fancy French press.

If I can get to the local restaurant where I live, The Country Cafe, I like to buy their dinner rolls for breakfast sandwiches. They are homemade and they bake them with the same dough that they use to make pizzas. They are absolutely the best. Being fresh made and not having a bunch of preservatives, I have to eat them within a day or so. I am not sure what preservatives they put in modern sliced bread, but the stuff will go from fresh, to stale and then remain dormant for a month, before becoming croutons. It does not mold. It might mold if you put it in a damp cellar. If I cannot get those rolls, I will sometimes go to Texas Roadhouse and get Chili and salad. They bring a whole basket of rolls. They are almost as good as the local rolls at the cafe. Of course, there is also the English muffins from the grocery store.

What do I like on a breakfast sandwich? I hit up any of the New England guys that are driving this way for field trials to bring linguica. It is a Portuguese sausage that I cannot find here in Pennsylvania. It can be bought in ground, links, or patties. The patties are great for breakfast sandwiches. I also cook venison patties from ground meat, but I add a lot of egg to the raw meat to prevent the low-fat venison from crumbling. Sure, there is also ham and whatever else I might get for the sandwiches. Sometimes I use scrapple, a Pennsylvania Dutch specialty that can be cooked crispy and works excellent on the Texas Roadhouse rolls.

All of this cooking occurs while I have beagles in the field, and there is a need for food security as strict as the measures that you might use while camping in grizzly country. What have I had beagles do while cooking outside?

My Lady Day, who passed away some years ago, actually learned how to open the refrigerator door. We had to install a child lock on the fridge just because of her. It worked well until my mother in law broke because it was apparently too difficult for her to figure out. Lady was also able to open a cooler. Of course, she could open the ones without a latch, but she was able to get into the coolers with the button on the handle that has to be depressed before it will slide open. I had tried to cook breakfast sandwiches several times before discovering a bloated Lady Day and an empty cooler.

I have a young dog now, Blitz, that opened a soft case cooler that has the lid close with a zipper. I presumed he would just shred the cooler, and it looks like he tried, but at some point, he figured out how to hold the cooler in place and move the zipper with his teeth. Pretty impressive really. Lady would be his great-aunt.

Night time cooking is another matter, and I will, at times, camp at a hunting spot or the beagle club. I run dogs until after dark, and then pick them up for the night. I make pizzas on fajita shells (using a frying pan), and will often opt for a wood fire, just for the benefit of smoke to chase away the bugs. It isn't a huge fire, but it keeps the skeeters away. Mountain pies are on the menu then. A mountain pie maker is basically a cast iron waffle maker with a long metal handle. You put bread in there and can make the contents a sandwich—meat and cheese—or dessert, with pie filling. I just put the iron in the fire, so to speak, and wait for it to brown on both sides. The sandwiches are great, and if you go to the city they charge a lot of money for a mountain pie and call it a panini. I then wake up in the morning and run the pack of beagles again.

It is a good way to get a mini-vacation. Go to the wild briars (or beagle club) after work, get a good bunny chase before going to bed. Then, get another chase in the morning, and go to work. Now, I will give you some real tricks that you can use for cooking outside and camping in the summer. Not the common-sense stuff about letting the meat rest, but some real tips that I have learned from camping as much as I do.

Corn on the cob is about as good as it gets for campfire food. Get a big mason jar (or ball jar) and put your butter into it. Cook your corn (hey, you can boil it or roast it, whatever you like) and when it is done, add hot water to your jar of butter. The butter will melt and rise to the top. Put the ear of corn in the jar and pull it up slowly, it will pass through the buttery top layer and coat the whole cob evenly.

I like open fires, but they have to be monitored and sometimes it is too dry to build one in the summer. I keep a propane stove for safe cooking in a dry season, and it is also fast heat. It ain't the most fun, has no ambiance, and sometimes I run out of fuel before I am done cooking because I try to get every last bit of gas out of the container. Yeah, I like an open fire at night, but almost always go for the contained flame from propane in the morning. I can drive away and not worry about smoldering coals, and I do not have to carry additional water to drench the coals.

I will also keep food with me that does not need to be cooked. If I get done exercising dogs and it is dark and raining, I do not want to stand around a fire and get drenched. I always have almonds and peanuts. I buy pistachios when they go on sale too. Jerky is a mainstay, and I make my own. Granola bars (adult candy bars) are commonly found in my truck console. Crackers and pepperoni are good options too. My wife gets the pepperoni made from turkey. It is healthier, and apparently, there is a lot of turkey meat not being bought, with the experts telling everyone how difficult it is to cook one. The turkeyroni, as I call it, is pretty good.

Doing dishes is part of it all, and I pack a gallon sized zip top bag with paper towels that have been coated in dish detergent. It takes up less space and just needs to have hot water to rinse. Better than paper towels, go to the auto-part-store and get those shop towels. Those things are heavy duty paper towels. Heck, you can almost reuse them they are so strong.

Condiments take up a lot of space. If you are taking your kids for fast food, grab some extra packets of mustard and ketchup while you are there. It takes up way less space and does not need to be refrigerated, leaving you the option of a smaller cooler. Oh, I get extra napkins while I am in there. At some point, while I am enjoying the beauty of nature, I find that nature calls. The same small shovel that we all carry to clean up after our dogs at a field trial is perfect for digging a hole for human waste. Burying it all ensures that no one has to have their beagles find your mess and paper and roll in it. I grab extra napkins everywhere I go, just in case I forget to take a roll of the soft stuff from the house.

Ever seen the canned dog food in the grocery store? I buy the Purina One. I keep some in the truck, just in case I forget to take kibble with me. If I feel that the canned food has been in the truck long enough that it has to be used, I will use it up and replace the cans. I am sure that canned stuff might last forever, but I do rotate the stock. I have also been known to mix it with dry food if I am getting low on the kibble during a three or four-day camping trip.

I hope to see you out there in the briars. For best results, take your family to a campsite where the cell phones don't work. Listen to hound music, eat some corn, and enjoy time away from digital-cyber-screen-electronic living. I have to go, my wife just said that she thinks Blitz has learned to open the refrigerator. I hope that youngster takes after his great-aunt in terms of rabbit chasing too.

AC

Last winter, there were days when the temperatures plunged and many people did not go rabbit hunting. Now, I know that this is *Better Beagling*, and our readers are more inclined to hunt in wintry conditions than most. Even so, we do have fellow beaglers who avoid the chill of winter. I tend to like the early spring field trials in Pennsylvania, where I live, because there is always a chance of snow, and that is when you can tell what dogs hunted for the past few months and which ones were in the kennel waiting for the field trial circuit to kick into gear again. I often say this and get some negative feedback.

"You know, just because you shoot a bunch of rabbits doesn't mean that you have great dogs!"

I hear that a lot. And I agree, to be honest. It does not take a great dog to have a fantastic hunting season. You just need dogs that can find rabbits, and not lose them. The great dogs can all do that and so much more. One thing about hunting, however, is that you can't be the sort of person who panics at the prospect of running dogs outside of a fenced enclosure, and you have to be sure that your dogs won't decide that a deer is better than nothing on a day when the rabbits are sitting tight and hard to find. In other words, the dogs have to handle well. While we emphasize that a dog has to hunt and search at a field trial, I sometimes wonder if we forget that hunting beagles have to hunt with us! I hunt a lot, and my dogs handle great, and part of the reason for that is that my pampered pooches live in the house and are pets. July is misery for my pack and me.

You see, I am not a fan of hot and humid weather. Last month, when the temperatures crept over 90 degrees, I had to take action. It was 3 o'clock in the morning and I was sweating. I moved my arm across the bed and noticed that my wife, Renee, was not under the bed sheets. Mind you, for the first two winters that she and I were married, I thought that she was actually cold-blooded. Not the type of cold-blooded person that does cruel and heinous things, but rather the kind of cold-blooded person that cannot generate her own heat. In the winter she would wear a sweater and a blanket while sitting in the living room. No, I didn't have the thermostat set and 65 degrees either. At least not after the first winter we were married.

"Are you trying to freeze me?" Renee asked that first year together.

"What?" I asked.

"It is only 65 in here."

"Just wear a long sleeve shirt," I shrugged as I was reading a book, without looking up.

"Are you kidding me!" she moved in front of me. She was wearing a hooded sweatshirt, "I am wearing a heavy shirt under this!" So, the thermostat is now set to 70 degrees, for my dear wife. I walk around in T-shirts and shorts through the winter.

Anyway, I was trying not to wake my wife while installing the air conditioner in our bedroom, last month. So, I did not turn on the lights. Our little window AC unit was in a small bedroom closet. I figured that I could get there in the dark and grab it easily. I am quite adept at getting around the bedroom in the dark, since I almost always take beagles afield before dawn, and that is hours before Renee prefers to rise. It works out well, however, since I am usually asleep by 9 o'clock at night, and she takes care of "last call." Last call is my language for the nighttime beagle drive. It is like a cattle drive, but you are forcing beagles to move. It happens after the 11 o'clock news when my wife has to drive the hounds into the yard to go pee before bedtime. They need to be forced because they prefer to snooze on the dog beds and blankets until after midnight, and then howl until one of us gets out of bed and lets them through the kitchen door, and into the fenced yard. More frequently than we like, the mutts will bark at things outside of the fence. The target of said cacophony can be rabbits, stray cats, skunks, opossums, raccoons, or the wind. A few times it has been a bear.

I, of course, take care of the first bathroom call in the morning. It's fair. I try not to wake her in the morning and she tries to let me sleep at night. While installing the air conditioner, I stubbed my toe on an exercise apparatus while getting into the closet. My wife has lots of things that are intended to make workouts fun and easy. They also double as drying racks for delicate fabrics that cannot go into the clothes dryer.

I then decided to carry the stupid air conditioner to the window, and in route, I stumbled on my slippers. This was a rookie mistake, as I usually put them on when I first wake up, but I often do not wear them when it is hot outside, because the bathroom floor can be as cool as it wants in the summer. The stumble sent me towards the bed, and I was very worried about dropping the 50-lb cooling device on Renee. So, I immediately leaned back so as to not fall forward, which would have plopped me and the air conditioner on her. I slumped to a halt against the cabinet that holds bed sheets, blankets, frilly things that run the perimeter of the bed, decorative pillows that get swapped on and off the bed at holidays and season changes, quilts, and some afghans—not the dogs, the skimpy-blanket-type-things with gaps in the stitching that look nice but are always to small. I landed with a thud, the air conditioner in my lap.

"I'm okay," I said. Renee snored. I moved to the window, adjacent to her side of the bed, and set the unit gently on the floor. I opened the window, and the blinds blew inward and rattled.

"Go make coffee, I'll be down soon," Renee sleep talked at the blinds. I thrust the machine into the window and almost dropped it to the sidewalk below since I was mistaken about the dimensions of the window's depth. I clung to the darn thing with my fingertips and said, "Renee, help me adjust this thing."

"Is the coffee done?"

"Wake up!"

"What?!"

44

"Help me get this!"

By that point, my fingers were about to give out, so I located the cord with my knee and grabbed it hastily. I hauled it back in as Renee bumped into me while getting out of bed, pushing me towards the open window.

"Jeez," I said.

"Well, what are you doing there in the middle of the night?"

"Trying to put in this blasted air conditioner!"

That was weeks ago, and now that we are in July, the hot days are more numerous. We have an AC unit in the living room too. The dogs snooze under it. And thump their tails whenever I am working on the computer or reading. The result is that we don't go afield as much right now. Whereas my beagles love the winter hunts and field trials with snow, they pant more and get hot faster than many dogs in the middle of the field trial season. So, we sit around and think cold thoughts. I keep blueberries in the freezer—it is better than ice cream. Speaking of cold treats, did you know that they sell ice cream for dogs? It is in the grocery store, and right next to the human ice cream. I once had a church member get it by accident, thinking it was for people, that is how I learned about it. I presume it is perfectly safe, but after finding the taste "off" for a few bowls, he looked at the container and discovered that it was, in fact, intended for dogs. I buy it for my mutts once in a while.

Last summer, Hoss (my high jumper) knocked the container onto the floor while I was answering the telephone, which had interrupted my dispersal of the cold snack. Then, as a combined unit, they engaged in a feeding frenzy, and they consumed the whole darn thing. You haven't seen anything until you have walked into your kitchen and seen your hunting pack on the floor, seemingly in medical distress. I knew the ice cream had no chocolate but could not determine the problem. Then I figured it out—they were writhing around with "ice cream headaches." They had front paws on their heads and were rolling on the linoleum while whimpering.

The forecast for tomorrow is for a cool front, and I am going to run dogs before dawn. It will be good to get out again, but I am still looking forward to winter. You'll see me afield more often after the cool morning dew returns, and the threat of frost is real. I won't wish away the fun of summer vacations, I will just dream about snow.

LET IT GO

There is never any shortage of people arguing about
lawn care. You can say some pretty outlandish things and
get away with it because lawns have become a veritable
religion. Take me, for instance, and my thoughts about
the lawn. To begin with, it seems that every time I decide
to be home, it rains. Cutting grass in the rain is not my
favorite thing to do, but sometimes it has to be done if the
meteorologists are constantly telling us that the skies are
going to open and the water is going to come out of the sky
in buckets. Do you have a neighbor that is out in the yard,
wearing rubber boots, and slogging the old lawn mower
through drenched, soaking wet, five-inch high grass? If so,
then you might live next to me. Sorry about that. Oh, and I
have added a new, even more humiliating dimension to my
lawn care practice. This is how it happened.

Do you remember, years ago, when they got rid of
all the good light bulbs? They gave us the energy saving
light bulbs, and I am pretty sure that a kerosene lamp
from the 1800s generated more light than those things.
The trade-off was that they would last for 14 years before
they burned out. Okay, I may be exaggerating there,
but they did promise some sort of remarkable lifespan
for these dim bulbs. At the time, I had a stockpile of the
rock and roll light bulbs. I call then rock and roll because
they burned hot and died young. But you could read a
book or thread a needle or do whatever other activity you
wanted in the middle of the night. I used them until they
were gone, and then I was forced into the energy saving
bulbs. I'll be honest, I almost became Amish. I am from
Pennsylvania, and it isn't unheard of to convert. I figured
I might be able to adapt to the lifestyle, and just do all my
reading in the daylight hours. Well, an Amish crew put
a roof on the neighbor's house, and they did not utilize

any power or pneumatic tools. They started stripping the roof when I went to work at 7 in the morning. When I came home from lunch they were putting down tar paper. When I returned at the end of the day they were finishing up the shingles. Four guys, with hammers, sounded like a drum roll they pounded the nails so quickly. I was so amazed that I walked over to see the whole production first hand. The leader of the crew extended me a business card and explained the rates, shaking my hand. The veins in his forearms looked as big as garden hoses, and the forearms themselves made Popeye look kinda scrawny. Any customer that decided to be underhanded with this crew better be glad that the Amish are pacifists because I would not want to try and keep up with those guys on a job or fight one of them.

So, I figured I would just have to use the energy-saving light bulbs; and continue upon my path of modern convenience, albeit inconvenienced by lower lumens. Then, they invented LED lights. I will be honest, I wasn't even aware that these lights were available for houses when they first arrived. I discovered them while in the hunting section of the department store. That is where I discovered these little lights that clipped onto the bill of a ball cap, weighed next to nothing, and generated a lot of light! I got them for running dogs in the morning before the sun rose, or catching dogs after sunset if I was conditioning dogs in the evening.

One day, I came home to see that my lawn was out of control and I was down to about 20 minutes of remaining daylight. I started mowing, knowing I could not get it finished, and then I remembered the LED light that clipped to my hat.

"What are you doing?" my wife rolled her eyes when she saw me going outside with the light.

"Mowing the grass why?"

"Normal people do not cut grass in the dark."

"Farmers work in the dark all the time," I said, "They make lights for tractors."

"You're a farmer now, huh?" she sighed.

"Well, no," I replied, "I'm just saying that if a farmer can harvest crops—his livelihood—in the dark, then why shouldn't I be able to trim this pesky yard?" And I did just that.

"You're an idiot," she told me as I walked into the house after putting the mower away.

"Why?"

"All the neighbors had their faces pressed up to their windows watching you push the mower back and forth."

"Yeah," I said with a grin, "I'm sure they were impressed. That was some real ingenuity."

"Yeah, more like amazed that somebody would ever do that," she said and walked away.

I love that LED light. And it truly is good for running beagles when you know you will start or end with an hour of darkness. Oh, and beagles are the reason why the grass gets out of hand. I have a neighbor that basically watches his lawn and waits for it to grow enough to cut. In his mind, the ideal time to cut it is when it has grown enough that you can barely see a few, sporadic puffs of green dust emerge from the "exhaust chute" that expels the cut grass from his garden tractor. There are definitely not enough clippings to be visible on the ground when he is finished. To be honest, I am not at all sure how he can tell where the mower has already cut, and where it needs to go next. Sometimes he mows every other day.

By contrast, my push mower is slinging gobs of battered grass that clumps on the ground like hay, waiting to dry in the sun. There is no doubt where the line of demarcation is between the part of the yard that I have mowed and the part that still needs mowing. Bushels of dead grass are strewn next to the 6-inch tall mix of weeds and grass that comprise my lawn. Yeah, I have weeds. Dandelions. Clover. Crabgrass. Stuff like that. My neighbors tend to wage war on their yards to eliminate all of those things.

Here's the thing, however. If I have a day with meetings, hospital visits, and bible studies, and two free hours, what do you think I will do? Yeah, I am going to run dogs. The lawn suffers. Next, you add a plan. Here is a typical plan: I see the weather forecast, notice that it is going to drizzle in the morning and then get sunny and hot. Okay, I take the beagles to see the bunnies before daylight and get home with the pooches a couple hours later. I then do visits, funerals, church work, or whatever is on my plate, and opt to come home before dark and mow.

At this time of year, it invariably will get hot, humid, and oppressive. Next thing I know there is a thunderstorm.

"Well," my wife will say, "The power is out again."

"I can't mow the grass now either," I reply.

"What are we going to do when it gets dark?"

"I suspect we won't have that much less light with the electrical grid down. These light bulbs are dreadful. But I have an LED light for my hat. So, I will probably cut the jungle in the dark." Obviously, that generates eye rolls. It is all because of the bunnies and beagles. I don't have time to attack dandelions. The funny thing is that there are varying thoughts on how to maintain the grounds of a beagle club too. Here in Pennsylvania, there are many clubs and most have a fence around them. Now, I will be the first to admit that we need to make sure that dogs can hunt rabbits, and therefore go into the wild. There was a time when you could not run dogs in the wild during the summer, and your club had to have a permit to do it. That meant a fence to make sure that your dog did not stray off the club property into land where dog training wasn't permitted in the summer. So, we have many clubs and most have fences, even now that we are allowed to train hunting dogs anywhere in the summer.

What crops do you plant? Clover? Switchgrass? How many grassy paths should you have? Most clubs have some paths for walking around, and other clubs have a lot more. The debate is whether the paths are good for generating food for rabbits, or whether the paths lack of cover makes it easier for hawks and owls to kill your bunnies. Once you decide how many paths you might want, a club has to decide how often to cut the grass. Some say that short grass is more nutritious for rabbits because it is tender and not as fibrous. Others feel that longer grass on those paths will help provide some cover from the aerial predators.

I took a church member to the beagle club because he wanted to see what all the fuss was about and why I trained beagles. He was very excited to see the dogs chase, and on morning dew the pack looked good. Hearing the beagles is always exciting and their voices echoed through the valley.

"This place has a lot of rabbits," he said, "And it looks like you let the place go and had the weeds take over."

"It takes a lot of work to get that look," I said, "Cuz if you let it go too long it turns into big trees." The dogs chased until dark, and I got my LED light to catch them. I went home and decided to cut my grass the next morning—while it was wet—to try and stunt its growth.

"Interesting strategy," the neighbor said.

"Yeah. It's organic." The neighbors are all about organic things.

"Oh," he said, "That is very good! It is a little long, almost like it got away from you, but I could see how you may have let it do that on purpose."

"I sure did," I bluffed.

"What school of lawn care is that?" he asked.

"It is based on biodiversity, wherein 'letting it go' fosters a more complex and interconnected ecology. It helps rabbits, insects, birds, all of the things you need to be more natural."

"I like it," he said and measured my lawn. "Four inches is your standard length before cutting?"

"You can go a couple more if you want," I said. I guess my yard care is based on a beagle club.

LET'S GO, SO WE CAN GET BACK

"Let's go," My dad said, "So we can get back!" Those were his words as we were on our way to get a pair of shoes since I had worn mine out. This wasn't something that he usually did—take me shopping for shoes—but Mom was busy taking care of her Mom that day, so my father had to do it since I needed the shoes the next day. Even if it wasn't something as detestable as shopping, Dad would often say "Let's go, so we can get back." He lived most of his life within a few miles of where he was born, with the exception of a tour with the Sea Bees in WWII when he went to the Philippine Islands. It wasn't as if he hated other places, it was just that he spent all his time at work or with his family. I suppose that I was the recipient of the bulk of his time since his outdoor hobbies were also my passions.

Keep in mind, he lived through the depression. So, it was his firm belief that every meal should have some meat. I never liked cube steak. Cube steak is still available in grocery stores, and it is basically bits of beef leftover from the butchering process that gets pounded into the shape of a steak. It's tough. I would rather have burger. In my dad's mind, cube steak was a bit better than burger. I suppose because it cost a bit more. But I would rather have anything made with hamburger—meatloaf, meat sauce over pasta, or a hamburger.

"You didn't eat your steak," he said to me.

"I had mashed potatoes and peas."

"You too good for cube steak?"

"I guess it is too good for me," I sighed, "I would rather have a burger." I could tell from the way he looked at me that I better eat it. As I ate the "steak" with three large glasses of water (I cut the meat into aspirin sized pieces and swallowed them whole with a gulp of tap water) I devised a plan to never have to do this again. I would feed it to the dogs. Now, I have done this countless times in my adult life, since my beagles live in the house. Oh, and my wife likes to experiment in the kitchen. I have palmed chicken as dry as the Sahara under the table to feed a pooch. I once pretended to spill pot roast onto the floor. Desperate times call for desperate measures.

The problem with Dad and the cube steak is that the dogs lived in a kennel, in the yard. So, I decided to never eat cube steak again, as I chased it with water like I was taking 200 pills. Speaking of water, it was tap water. For younger readers, I want you to be aware that there was a time when we drank the water that came out of the kitchen sink. I don't think bottled water even existed then, except for fancy stuff that no one bought. If you would have told me then that people would pay as much money for water as they spend for soda pop or iced tea, I would have never believed it. Alas, that is the way it was.

Anyway, about halfway through the steak and part ways into a freshly filled glass of water, I decided that what I needed to do was sneak the meat into a container—probably on my lap or under the table—and then whisk it away to the hounds. A couple of months later, I had the opportunity, and I wore a hooded sweatshirt to supper, which was fine since it was winter. I had lined the entirety of my sweatshirt's pocket (it was one pocket with openings on either side) with saran wrap. All I had to do was sneak the steak into my pocket. It worked, remarkably well. When I went outside to feed the dogs after supper, I added the cube steak to their fare. I did this every time Mom served cube steak, until I moved out to college, and never got caught.

Fast forward to my tenure as a stepfather and things look a little differently. My wife, Renee, occasionally has to go to work-related conferences. At first, I thought that these were conferences of the sort where she was in long meetings and had to learn lots of things. It turns out that most of them are at Disney, and the others are in Las

Vegas. Renee's social media is full of pictures of her with Mickey Mouse and selfies of her gal friends eating dessert. At any rate, on those instances, I had to take care of feeding my stepson, Wesley, and myself. I decided not to subject him to the cube steak, so I would cook kid-friendly food.

"I don't want spaghetti!" he yelled.

"Then why did you tell me that you wanted spaghetti earlier?" I asked.

"That was a long time ago."

"It was two hours ago."

"I don't want spaghetti anymore."

I can assure you that if I had requested a meal and then refused to eat it, I would have sat at the table until I ate it willingly or my father force fed me. That being said, I figured I would play it cool. "Then you can eat whatever you want that is in this house," I said, "Cereal, sandwiches, those frozen pizzas you like, or whatever." To be honest, I didn't care if he ate potato chips. Twenty minutes later, my cell phone rang. It was Renee. "What is going on with supper?" she asked.

"Wes asked for spaghetti and then refused to eat it."

"You need to order him Chinese food," she said.

"Why?"

"Because that is what he wants."

"You are breaking up," I lied, "I will take care of it."

I walked over to Wes and said, "You can call your mom all you want. But I am not having two separate meals for two people." By day three of her conference in Florida, the kid was eating what I cooked. I was simply amazed that it took him that long to be happy with a meal that he requested!

There is this process that we go through when it comes to our dad. Little kids are convinced that their own father is the best father there is and ever has been. Granted, this isn't true for kids that have abusive parents or absentee dads. As teens, kids start to realize that Dad isn't necessarily the greatest guy on earth, and this leads to a late teen/early twenties assertion that their dad is a complete idiot. Gradually, people tend to gain balance and realize that their parents are people, like everyone else, and have strengths and weaknesses, like everyone else. Wes is 22 years old now. And yes, I am a complete moron. For the most part, I am okay with being a moron. I do not mind when he insults me as he "fixes" my computer.

"Why does it start on Calibri font?" I said, "I hate Calibri. Why do I have to manually change to Times New Roman?"

"You have to set the preferences," Wes said.

"Yeah," I sighed, "Can you just do that for me?"

"I guess," he groaned and in 4 clicks he remedied the situation and walked around like he was taking care of an invalid. "I can't believe you can't do that," he said.

I wanted to say, "I can't believe you can't drive my truck because it is a manual transmission," but I did not want to hurt his feelings. He can't take teasing like kids once endured from their parents.

For instance, my own father once told me, "You're a smart kid, but you have zero common sense. You better go to college, because I don't know how else you will make it in this world."

I should clarify, that "smart" is not necessarily a compliment in my family, as it is akin to smart-aleck. Also, a lack of common sense was virtually synonymous with imbecile. In other words, there were lots of book smart people who lacked the skills to fix their own car or build their own house. My dad built several houses, and when I was a youngster he put a foundation under the house we lived in. He had bought the house for cheap—since it was in disrepair, and he remodeled it. He decided that it needed a full cellar, instead of just sitting on stones. So, he put the house on jacks, and we hand-dug the cellar. It was solid clay. I was in that hole all summer—maybe 12 years old— swinging a pick.

"You got a good swing boy," Dad teased, "If that book learning doesn't work out, you have a heck of a career ahead of you in manual labor." He poured one wall of cement at a time. Cement trucks would drive up to the house, and the walls would be poured through chutes that entered our house and into holes he cut in the floor.

It took all summer to dig, but when it was done the house was perfectly level. I marvel at it now, but I had no doubts that Dad could build anything. He put his tools in the basement, and a wood stove to heat the whole house. At night, Dad and I would sit down there and talk. We would feed the wood fire in the winter. We would escape the heat in the summer. He felt the house needed that cellar to be home. We lined the walls with canning shelves to be stockpiled from the garden.

This brings me back to "Let's go so we can get back." Dad loved home. And the routines of home. This always included beagles. The routines of feeding and watering the hounds are built into the very fabric of the day. Chasing rabbits isn't a chore, but it isn't optional either. You run rabbits because that is the whole reason that you own beagles. That routine was vital in my childhood.

"We have to go to a luncheon today," my wife said the other week, "It is for a work colleague. She is moving to a new job and is having a gathering at her house."

"What time?" I asked.

"Noon," Renee answered.

I calculated that we would be there for three hours. It might be a half hour drive home, depending on traffic. So, it might be 3:30 or even 4:00 by the time we got home. But, if I got home at four o'clock, I could definitely run dogs for a few hours before dark. It wouldn't be a totally ruined Saturday.

"Okay," I said, "Let's go, so we can get back." Happy Fathers' Day.

Summer Break

It seems like a long time ago, but I still recall the joy, the fantastic happiness that goes with the last day of school. June is here, and school will soon be out for the year. Parents can't wait to stop having the morning battles with their kids. My stepson, Wesley, was a particularly difficult kid to wake up in the morning. I was famous for pouring cold water on his hair, which had great success. His mother, my wife, always reacted negatively to this tactic. She felt that the cold water on the hair was just shy of waterboarding a prisoner. Although I no longer have a kid in school, I can tell you that I will be happy to not see school buses in the morning.

If I try hard, I can remember the last day of school. Let's face it, there was no education happening that day. You were there for a few hours, fed an early lunch, and sent home. It was the 180th day, the minimum number of days that could comprise a school year in Pennsylvania. The whole day had the feeling that the inmates were running the prison. Teachers were just keeping kids from going too far. You could talk all you wanted and I remember the last day being loud.

I didn't pay much attention to it, but I seem to recall a sense of relief for the teachers as well. They had made it through another year. They had dealt with another crop of troublemakers, slow learners, overachievers, and brownnosers. The whole day bred enthusiasm that peaked on the last bus ride of the year. Those poor drivers.

Kids screamed at the top of their lungs. "No more pencils no more books no more teachers' dirty looks!" Even as the bus emptied, and there were far fewer students on board, the shouts were deafening. The driver moved a little faster, revved the engine a little higher, and finished the route a little faster. And then we were paroled. For a summer. Out of school for a few glorious months. The best summers were the years between the ages of thirteen and fifteen. I was old enough to go do a lot of things, but still too young to get a full-time job. Thirteen was also the age when I got my first beagle.

I was obsessed with chasing rabbits, and not much has changed. Dad and I would take the beagles to the beagle club every morning. Well, most mornings. Some days he worked first shift, and he couldn't go. Usually, he worked second or third shift. When you go every day, the dogs get used to it. They would howl in the kennel, waiting for us to load them into the truck. The neighbors must have hated this. The people living around us were retired, and the morning chases were a disturbance. It awakened some, and just annoyed others. Imagine, you have your windows open to let the cool morning air roll into your house, and you hear the nonstop baying of beagles that are trying to leave for the briars a little earlier today than they did yesterday.

On the mornings when there wasn't much dew, I would wear my "school sneakers." That was the pair of sneakers that were specifically reserved for school, the pair that I had to take off as soon as I got home, and then wear an older, dirtier pair. I could wear any pair I wanted once the school year ended. The same was true for my pants and shirts. I am being serious when I tell you that I do not recall ever seeing a tick—no wood ticks, dog ticks or deer ticks. And I was outside from dawn until dark.

Back then, it was illegal to train dogs in the summer, at least here in Pennsylvania. Well, you could train dogs, but it had to be at a beagle club. The idea was to let the rabbits breed and not bother them with dogs. My whole day revolved around getting to the beagle club. Dad and I would go most mornings, and then I would beg a ride to go back in the evening. I would ask grandma, my uncle, Mom, my neighbor, other club members, whoever would get me there! Somehow I always got there. It was only a few miles away, and I did not realize then how lucky I was to live that close to a club. I have never lived closer than a ½ hour from a club since then. Dad always made sure I could go, even when he was working. He would even let me run dogs at night. I was allowed to stay at the club until midnight. If I went into town, I had to be home by 9!

The last day of school is different now. I saw kids get off the bus with no yelling. They were all staring at their phones, their necks almost seemed to be forming a hump form the constant bending to see the screens. They go outside less too. no doubt the fear of ticks is part of the reason why they do not go, but the phones also keep them in constant communication with their friends. We had to roam around and find our friends. I would bring the beagles home from the woods by nine o'clock in the morning and then find friends. We might play baseball. If there were only three of us, we would play catch or trap. Trap is also called pickle, and we would have two bases and a guy with a glove at each. A runner would get between the bases and try to make it safely to one of them.

There was always fishing, and long after the cool spring days passed into hot summer, we would try to coax a trout to take a hook. When the water was low, we would wade into the stream and retrieve lures that were lost to limbs and other snags. We would try to get our own lures back, but we would also acquire new ones. Legion League baseball games were a prime attraction. We would climb the trees outside the center field fence in order to see the final resting spot of a home run. Then we would run after them. This was how we replenished our own supply of baseballs, which was always low.

Of course, the end of school led to the wonder about the beginning of the new school year. Who would you get for homeroom teacher? What girls were breaking up with their boyfriend and might be available to date? How would the football team be? Football seemed to be a year-round enterprise. Eventually, however, there were no more last days of school. You graduated. Even if you went to college or trade school, there would never be a last day of school like you experienced in elementary and high school. You could choose your life after you graduated high school. Prior to that, you were navigating as best you could, and having to do so within the confines of the system.

So often, we hear that high school is the best days of our lives. My response is always, "If the best days of my life involved raising my hand to go pee, then that doesn't say much." It is easy to forget about that. Or the bullies. Bullies were a real thing then, and at some point, you would be in a fist fight with one. It is easy to forget that there were times when being popular was a concern. Well, maybe you didn't need to be popular, but you definitely did not want to be unpopular. Remember the unpopular kids, who were maligned and teased for years before they graduated?

When I think back, I mostly remember the school year starting and then glorious autumn. Skipping school a few times to hunt rabbits, and then there was deer season, well that was closely followed by Christmas. There was rushing home to go trout fishing in the spring, and back then, before the National Wild Turkey Federation, you might get a spring gobbler, but they were so rare that if you saw a turkey track in the mud you would be a legend. Nowadays, I routinely stop my truck as I wait for dozens of turkeys to cross the road, single file, looking at me as if I were a nuisance on their morning commute for grasshoppers. Then, after all that, it was summer. For those of you that have kids or grandkids in school, be sure to enjoy these summers. Take those kids to a few trials, and more importantly let them just run the hounds. It won't be long before those kids are graduating. Hopefully, we can keep some kids in this lifestyle of chasing rabbits and hare with beagles. The more I see the bent necks and the cell phones as they get off the bus, the more I worry. I don't blame the kids; we parents are as much to blame as anyone.

You never know when helping a kid catch a fish, shoot a turkey, or chase a rabbit with a beagle will change everything. Obviously, I was taught many things in school to graduate. History, math, science, and more were required classes. Mostly, looking back on childhood, I remember beagles. They have made all the difference in my life. At some point, early in this month, I am going to sneak off to the woods for a few days without any people. Just me and the beagles. I want to try and remember more fully the joy that came with the last day of school, which was always in June for my school district. When I was 16 I started working every summer, full-time. That is why I previously said that my best summers lasted until I turned 15 years old. I feel that I must find some way to have that feeling of a summer that exists just for fun. Even if just for a few days.

COMMONPLACE

Not too many months ago, I was walking around a local park with a little pup, because the place is full of rabbits. It isn't the kind of park that has a playground, but rather a paved bike trail and a bunch of brush inside of it. I was the only one in the brush. You can't hunt there, so the rabbits were sort of tame and would let a pup bump right into them. Naturally, people thought I was crazy. I mean, it was in State College, PA where I sometimes have to go to work, and being a college town there just aren't many people engaged in outdoor sports, at least by percentage. Well, you can find an abundance of fishermen, but to fit in you have to own a fly rod. It would help if the fly rod was made of bamboo and cost upwards of $3,000.00 too. Naturally, you need to drive to the stream (they never say creek, and if they do they pronounce wrong. It is pronounced crick!) in a vehicle no less expensive than a Land Rover. The luxury model. Preferably, you should get something a little swankier than that, but you definitely need a fancy set of wheels. Lastly, you must never eat a fish, but rather, you catch and release only. Where was I? Oh, yeah, it isn't a hunting crowd.

So, as I was walking onto the path with a pup on a leash, they all looked at me funny. At first, I thought it was because I was not carrying a plastic bag to gather puppy poo and take it home, which is the park rule. No worries, he did his business in the briars like all dogs should do. No, I think they were looking at me weird because they could tell that the cute bundle of beagle puppy was going to become a hunting dog. Meanwhile, no one bothered to notice the complete nut that was hurtling towards us in a sprint. While pushing a baby stroller. Yep, he had a sporty stroller of some sort, big wheels (only 3 of them), low center of gravity and a rugged frame.

"That pup is cute," he paused to pet Blitz.

"Yeah," I said, "Which is good, considering how mischievous he is."

I looked at the baby in the stroller. She looked terrified, no doubt because she was just whipping down the trail at a sprint. I mean, it's one thing to put a car seat in the back of your enclosed car, but this poor kid must've been feeling the velocity and turns. Her eyes were bugged out and her head was still kind of bobbing around.

Just then, the baby started to cry. "I think I scared your baby," I said.

"No, she does that whenever I stop running he said, as he adjusted his spandex pants and stretched his legs.

"She cries when you stop?"

"Yeah," he said and started pushing the stroller down the path. I suddenly had a memory of holding my niece when she was young, and when she was wanting to cry I would toss her a few inches into the air and catch her. The sensation of moving upward was enough to quell her urge to cry, I think because she was scared. I only did it a few times to get her back to her mother. For some reason, I had the thought that perhaps that young baby in the stroller was terrified the entire time she was speeding down the path, and started to cry whenever the sensation of moving stopped. I watched the stroller whisk out of sight and thought I saw that it had a rugged suspension, like an off-road vehicle or something.

I simply cannot imagine my father paying for a jogging stroller. I am sure the price would be problematic, but most of his running was in the woods and going over downed trees and between brush piles. No stroller could make it. In fact, I do not recall going too many places with my dad until I could keep up with his long legs. It is a whole different era, in terms of parenting.

I never was taken on a playdate. By contrast, my stepson, Wesley, seemed to always have to have time with friends officiated by his mother or me. I remember driving to his friends' houses and supervising while the kids played.

"Do we all have to babysit or can some of us go home?" I asked one time.

"You can't be serious," a mother sighed.

"Why?"

"Well, we all have to be here to discipline our own children."

"Why?" I asked again.

"What if Wesley misbehaved and you weren't here?"

"Well," I said, "You can yell at him anytime you want."

"Can you make sure that your wife brings Wesley from now on?"

"Absolutely," I said.

As I recall childhood, we kids did the chores we were asked to do and then disappeared before we were asked to do more. You would ride your bicycle to several locations, looking for friends. There was the ballfield, the creek, and the woods beyond the edge of the neighborhood. You would rendezvous with your buddies in one of those places. It wasn't planned, and we didn't phone each other to plan it. We just found one another and commiserated.

"Man," you might say, "The only thing worse than picking all those peas is knowing that I have to eat them tonight."

"How about it?" a friend would nod, "My dad has me scraping the porch to paint it."

We spent hours each day intentionally not being visible, so as to not get additional tasks assigned by being at home, and underfoot. Parents, for their part, had a nonbinding contract, to simply ignore us until we got hungry enough to come home. Naturally, they might come looking for you if something popped up. It was always a bad sign when your mom went driving around town looking for you. It was worse when Dad showed up. Mom might be bringing good news on a rare instance. Dad was there to rain on your day. For instance, my mom once found me to let me know that the new baseball glove I ordered had arrived since she knew I was waiting for it. It arrived COD, which seems crazy to people now. Basically, you paid a couple dollars extra but you could order an item and not pay for it until it arrived. It was perfect for kids without bank accounts. I just counted up the money that I had made and gave it to my mom to pay for the glove when it arrived.

Dad found me one time to tell me that the school had called and informed him that I had gotten in trouble the day before. His old International pickup truck pulled up, he rolled down the window and yelled, "You're done playing with your friends. I'll see you at home," he said, and I knew that I was about to be in worse trouble than the school had given me. Speaking of school, it was not too common for my dad to disagree with the school on matters like this. My stepson, on the other hand, had many incidents at school where his mother and I would make an argument on his behalf. We would descend upon the school like attorneys, to file our appeal against the school.

"I see here that Wesley flunked this test," my wife, Renee, said.

"Yes he did," his teacher replied.

"Are you aware that he had been sick and absent before this test was administered?" Renee rebutted.

"Yes," the teacher replied, "He missed two days the week before the exam."

"Can't he get a second chance?"

"The test covered material from the last month. Those two days were hardly enough to be the cause of the failing grade."

I could not imagine my father going to the school to argue that I needed special treatment. "Why didn't you have somebody tell you the homework assignments from the days you were sick? Are you an idiot?" is the sort of question I would receive in a situation like that. Yet, my dad was good to me. He emphasized work, but he firmly believed that I needed to have fun. "I will give you all the responsibility that you can handle, and then you can have all the fun you want."

This was most powerfully true when it came to the beagles. He would let me skip school to hunt rabbits if my grades were good. He would go afield and run dogs with me every evening when he worked any shift other than 3-11. In the summer, when there was no school, we would load up the dogs every morning, except on weeks he worked 7-3. When I was a teenager, we would be awake early, talking as the dogs chased. My friends tended to sleep in on summer days before we were old enough to have jobs at a store or business. I guess I was always a morning person, like my dad. I learned how to drive on the dirt road and grass parking lot of the beagle club—when I was still too young to legally drive on the road.

Always we were watching the dogs chase. We would get in front of them and see the rabbit, and then we would evaluate the dogs based on what we saw them do.

"You can't tell what they are doing with your ears only," he said. We would watch the dogs move into the brush and then we would find another place to intercept the rabbit and see what the dogs were doing. "It sounds like that dog is getting the check," he pointed, "Because he barks first when the pack loses the scent trail. But he is thinking out loud. Princess is always the second dog barking at a loss, but she is the first one solving it. He is just barking out of excitement while he watches her." Of course, we talked about more than dogs. It was about life and death. Goals, and dreams. Plans, and backup plans. Winning and losing.

Dad has been gone since 1991. I have been hunting rabbits and hare as far west as Montana, and as far East as Maine. I have hunted in Alabama and a lot of places in between. I know that my life with hounds has happened because of my dad. I try not to let Father's Day be sad, just for that reason. I wish I realized how important our time in the field was when it was happening. All those hours, that were so formative in who I became, seemed commonplace. I guess that's the way of it when you parent properly. All the important things seem commonplace. When in fact, they are not.

SELF-ESTEEM

May is the last month of school in many places, though it may continue into June a few days. I was surprised to learn that it is also Teen Self-Esteem Month. The reason that I was surprised, is because when I was a teenager the presumption was that teens had too much self-esteem, also known as hubris. Let me give you a for instance.

When I was a teenager I would carry four bags of dog food at once. This was back when all dog food companies sold it in fifty-pound bags. I would put one bag on each shoulder, and carry one in each hand. It was easy. Just for the record, they were probably 55-pound bags. Anyway, I would do that at the beagle club of my youth and the old-timers would say, "You are doing good, but any kid your age can do that."

Do you see how that is not a compliment? It just means that any buffoon can carry dog food. This was back when a kid like me, who didn't make varsity sports, was still forced to do tough time in chores. My dad was a firm believer that kids should work. Firewood was a big part of my life. Naturally, I appealed to my mom for help. "Mom," I said, "I have split enough wood for this winter and next. Can't you put a good word in for me? Maybe Dad will let me get a break?"

"Sure," she said, "I already cleared it with him. You are free from wood. You will work for my mom."

My Gram was a tyrant. She always had a plan to survive the next Great Depression. She lived through The Great Depression and was convinced that it was coming back to wipe us all out. So, she made her grandkids gather food. There were fiddleheads in the early spring, wild leeks in April, and berries all summer. By the time I was 15 years old, she had acquired 3 freezers. These were all kept full of food. In the spring, I was sent to catch trout. Trout were both wild and tame. The tame trout were stocked by the state for people to catch with ease, and the wild ones were found high in the hills. She would send me to catch the tame ones first.

"Don't come home without a limit!" she would yell. The tame trout were fed pellets all year where they were raised, and I would catch them with cork, cut to look like the pellets the fisheries fed them. I would go to the neighbor and beg for his corks and cut them into the same shape as the pellets that were fed to the farm-raised trout. The pellets looked like Tylenol capsules.

"Hey George," I'd yell from the porch.

"What?" George would yell from inside his house, his screen door locked but letting the wind inside.

"I need some cork!" I would yell.

George walked to the door. Actually, he staggered. "Is there enough on the porch?" he said.

A quick look showed dozens of wine bottles strewn across the porch floor. A closer examination revealed the corks, which he had thrown into the far corners, and stepped upon.

"Yeah," I said, "I can use those!"

"Good," he said, "Come back later. I need you to deliver some things."

"Okay!" I yelled.

I took the corks, made some "feed pellets" and caught trout. I caught my limit and returned home. My Gram said, "Well, not bad, but they are all barely big enough to be legal."

Fast forward to my early days as a step-father. My stepson, Wes, caught a trout. One trout. This was with every bait known to modern science. "Nice job!" I shouted.

"What?" my wife, Renee, standing next to us, said to me.

"I congratulated him," I said.

"Not enough!" she fumed.

"What do you mean?" I asked.

"He has been trying for three weeks to catch that trout," she whispered in my ear.

"I know," I said, "I think that trout he caught might be brain damaged."

"You need to make a bigger fuss," she whispered and waved her arms. I looked her in the eyes. Her eyes were serious.

"Gee whiz, lad," I exclaimed, "That is the biggest fish I ever saw!" I grabbed the 8" trout and put it on the bank.

"Really?" he yelled.

"Sure," I said, "I have never seen one like it!"

Back in my youth, the tame trout would be caught, and the weather would get hot. The only remaining trout were found high in the hills, in spring-fed streams that stayed cold all summer and remained ice-free all winter. Gram sent me there next, and if it was still spring, I could run beagles. I would run the dogs all morning while I tried to catch a few trout. One shadow across the water scared them away. One cast that made a big ripple ended your day. It was all about stealth. The dogs chased in the distance, and I tried an assortment of bait—corn, crawfish tails, worms, and live minnows. Minnows worked best. I would come home with three wild, savvy trout. Maybe just two. Sometimes, only one.

"Not bad," she would say. That was high praise. She would fillet them and put them in the freezer.

"I had trouble catching the dogs," I told Gram, "They ran deep into the hemlocks."

"You should have left them at home," she said, "It's fishing season, not rabbit season.

This is the way it was. "I see you got all As and a B on your report card," My Mom said to me one time.

"Thanks," I said.

"What's up with the B?" Mom asked, "It was in Reading class? You read all the time. You should've got an A there too."

Self-esteem was seen as a sin, really. You should always do better. That was what confused me when I got married. My stepson went to high school with constant monitoring. Had we wanted to, we could track what classroom he was in, what tests he took, and where he went wrong. I never tracked him on the computer, as I could have done, in part because I did not know how to do it. But the school called at times. And sent emails. One day, I got two emails. One said he was flunking two classes at the midpoint of the grading period. The other said that He owed money in the cafeteria. He was eating $7 dollars of food per day, and apparently flunking quizzes.

"School sent emails," I told my wife.

"What did they say," she said.

"Apparently, his best class is lunch," I shrugged my shoulders.

"Well," she said, "You support him and say something nice.

"Okay," I said.

Wes got home from school, and I said, "You're a good eater lad, that's good Keep getting nutrition." This was also when he got certificates every day, celebrating every achievement. He got ribbons too. I took him fishing one day for stocked trout, and I tore apart an old cork bulletin board to make bait.

"What are you doing?" he said.

"I am making a lure to look like the food they feed tame fish," I said. I took him out and he was catching fish left and right with the cork. Beagles chased in the background.

I started to think about George. How he made me go back to his house after I took his corks. When I got to his house, he gave me bottles of homemade wine to deliver to people in the neighborhood. They gave me money, and I took it back to George. There was grape wine, dandelion wine, strawberry wine, and others. It took three hours to do it.

"Here's the money," I told George.

"Thanks," he said, and gave me $10.

It seems surreal now. A little kid, running beagles, delivering wine, and catching trout. I was still thinking it over when Wes tugged on my arm, "Look at that trout!" he said.

"Man, that is a whopper," I said.

"Biggest you ever seen?" he grinned a smile that lacked a few teeth.

"You bet," I said. I am not sure where all this self-esteem is leading us, but at least he never delivered wine as a minor to fill his grandma's freezers.

CAMPFIRES

One of the great things about spring is campfires. I find campfires to be one of the best occasions for building community. Not too long ago, I was invited to a dinner party. It was at a house owned by friends of my wife. For reasons that I cannot altogether identify, my wife, Renee, feels a constant need to set me up on playdates to talk with her friends. Well, more specifically, her friends' husbands. Typically, we do not have much in common. At this last dinner party, we walked into the house and were confronted by a game on the television and music in the kitchen. People watched the baseball game, and they roamed into the kitchen for food. The two things fought for the attention of your ears. I smelled burgers. There was a small fire in the backyard, and it drew my attention. I walked outside, leaving the ball game and the music behind. It was the best place at the dinner party. I volunteered to help cook the burgers and bratwurst since the host was busy entertaining. I told jokes, and a crowd gathered that told their jokes.

"Where have you been," Renee said as she walked up to me in the yard.

"Right here."

"Of course you found the fire," she rolled her eyes at me.

"They needed help," I said, "And they didn't have an ax to split more wood. I had one in the truck."

"Oh," she said, "I know. Ever since you and Cody got barricaded into the woods, you carry an ax or saw to cut downed trees on roads."

"How did the people that live here get firewood without an ax?" I asked.

"Shh," she hushed me, "Some people just get wood delivered and don't have an ax." I blinked in disbelief and then quartered another round of wood.

72

"Whoo!" the suburbanites yelled as I heaped more wood on the fire.

I've always been pretty good at building fires, this dating back to my childhood when I would have to start a fire in the wood furnace for heat in the winter. Well, in the fall and spring too. Sometimes you would go past our house and all the windows were open to cool it down to 80 degrees. An outdoor fire, however, is one of my favorite social events. Can you imagine how long we have been doing this? Since we were cavemen. Since our hunting dogs were still mostly wolf. Heat. Light. Sparks to keep the dangerous critters away.

I am not fond of huge bonfires that are unapproachable. I like a fire that gives light and warmth. When I was a kid, my beagles lived in a kennel. In the spring, I loved to build a fire in the backyard fire pit and nod off to sleep with the beagles on my lap. There's just something about the crackle and hiss of the fire that comforts me.

At field trials, the campfire is the best part of the gathering. Sure, guys are still competitive about ribbons. Naturally, there is a debate about dogs. But there is also the focus that a fire brings. Especially if you are at a club with poor cell phone reception. The dinner party had television and music. It is the singular focus of the campfire that I like. Maybe the low light adds to the whole thing. The focus naturally turns to spoken words, and words heard. Almost 20 years ago, at a campfire at Corning Beagle Club, Roger Alderman was talking about a wasp nest in a tree, "A kid got stung today," he said on the night after the first day of the trial.

"Just cut it down," I said.

"What do you mean," Roger grinned. If you knew Roger, he always grinned.

"My dad would cut the limb holding the nest into a plastic garbage bag," I said, "I held the light for him. He'd tie the bag and double bag it and throw it in the garbage."

"Well," Roger said, "You are doing that tonight."

"Sure," I said, but you gotta hold the light."

We walked up to the bush that held the wasp nest, and I put the bag under the hive. I used pruning shears to cut the limb and—it was suddenly very dark. I looked up and Roger was running much faster than I thought a guy his age could run. I saw the light bobbing away from me. I tied the bag and heard the wasps buzzing a little, but not much. I sat in pitch black until my eyes acclimated to the darkness enough to walk.

"Why'd you leave me?" I asked Roger when I returned.

"I thought I heard a bee," He grinned.

If I am honest, there is no better feeling than having the side of your body facing the fire feeling way too hot, and the side of your body facing away feeling cold. When your face feels like it is sunburned from the fire, and you turn around that is the best. Your face feels soothed by the cold air as you turn, and your backside is delighted to have the flames throw some *Fahrenheits* in your direction. Yes, I just made up the word "Fahrenheits" to describe a volume of warmth thrown towards you.

Naturally, the campfire is good for running dogs. You can't see the dogs, and you can't evaluate them well in the dark. I think the dogs know this to be true. They just chase with no concern about ribbons or comparison. Andy Purnell and I would run dogs in the dark. We talked about dogs and listened to the chase. Until quitting time. He had all his dogs trained to leave a chase and come to him when he toned them with his handheld. I stumbled into the dark with a flashlight to catch them. There were a few chases that found me with only a cellphone flashlight to see the hounds as they rushed across a path in a blur. I would dive, get muddy, tear clothes, and eventually catch my dogs. Andy sat by the fire and waited for me. He'd yell, "You okay?" every ten minutes. But he didn't come out to help me. Porcupines and skunks are the downside of night running, but the problem can be minimized in grounds that get lots of night chases.

I am not sure that food gets any better than when cooked over the open fire. mountain pies, burgers, whatever. When I was a kid, we would build a fire at night and wander towards field corn in adjacent farms. Field corn, if cooked immediately, is almost as good as sweet corn. We would shuck it, put it in aluminum foil, and throw the ears near the fire. Every once in a while, we would roll them to ensure even cooking. Otherwise, we would just talk about the hunting trips we would one day make, girls we would one day date, and jobs we would one day have. Oh, and try to figure out how to fix our trucks. We all drove used beaters that required almost daily maintenance.

A winter fire is almost too serious. You need it to survive. I have had a couple of incidents wherein I was forced to build a fire and stay there, sleepless, until the dawn. Feeding the fire as best I could to stay warm as I worried about how far I was from where I should be. Then, with light, I could find my way out of the woods. A summer fire is almost a burden. I have been to beagle clubs in August, a raging fire adding to the misery of high temperatures and higher humidity. I like fall and spring for campfires.

Of course, the smoke follows you and there isn't much you can do about that. But even that, in mosquito season, can be a comfort. All of our homes have a fire in them so that we stay warm in winter. Maybe you have fuel oil or natural gas, and you don't typically see the flame, but there is a fire burning in your house! This is all too certain when we realize that most house fires are in the winter, during the heating season. Fire is dangerous. How else could you tell ghost stories, other than around a fire?

I suppose an old man could give us sound wisdom by sending it to us by group email, but it just seems more appropriate if he gives that wisdom to us in small, chunky segments as he pokes the fire with a stick to aerate it. What kind of wisdom? I have heard all sorts of good advice from a campfire.

"Good dogs get better the longer they are dead. You forget their faults."

"You realize that saying your opinion louder doesn't make it more true?"

"You can watch a thief, what do you do with a liar?"

"A dog that is faulty and one that is rabbit wise aren't the same thing, but they look it."

"You're saving nickels and spending dimes."

"You have a dog's entire life to get faulty, why hurry in its derby year?"

"Getting old ain't for sissies."

"Statues shoot rabbits. Be still."

"Changing your mind isn't flip-flopping when you get new information. It is learning."

Of course, there is much more. See you at the campfire. Paul Blossom is bringing pallets.

PAPER ROUTES, BEAGLES, AND MOM

Certainly, mothers are different than fathers, in most cases. For instance, when my own mother was wanting me to alter my behavior, she would give me to the count of three. "One," she would start. I often continued with my bad behavior. "Two," she would say next. If I did not respond, we got into math lessons. "Two and a half . . . two and three-quarters . . . two and seven-eighths . . ." She never broke it down into sixteenths. So, when she counted to three, she was really counting to six. Then, there were consequences. Sometimes, I still shudder to see a wooden spoon. But she gave a grace period.

One time, when I was about five, I made a mess in the living room by scattering matchbox cars everywhere. My mother was in the process of counting to three when my father walked into the room and planted his foot on one of those metal cars. It jammed into his foot. He grabbed me by the arm, gave me a mediocre swat on the behind and said, "Pick them all up now before it gets worse for you." He walked away muttering, "Why is she counting in fractions?"

The other thing my mother would do to let me know I was in trouble was call me Robert, instead of Bob. And if she added the middle name with it, I knew it was serious. When I was 12 years old, I got a paper route. It was *The Erie Sunday Times* and was my first real income. Sure, I had friends that earned an "allowance" for doing chores, but my own father felt that chores were one of the main reasons that a person had kids. I took the route from an older kid, a teenager, and he had not put too much effort into the route in recent years. The first thing my mother did was to build the route. Mom was a social butterfly. She met her friends, they had gatherings. If my memory serves me correctly, she went to "Tupperware parties" wherein other moms sold Tupperware to each other. Oh, and my mom cut hair. She went into the homes of elderly ladies who could not get out anymore and would "set" their hair every week.

"You are getting up earlier for papers this week," Mom said to me after I had the route for three weeks.

"Why?" I asked.

"I got you ten new customers."

"That's great," I said, "Thanks."

Well, let me tell you, in no time at all I was delivering well over 150 Sunday Papers. This, by the way, was before cable news. Well, there may have been CNN in the cities, but those of us without cable didn't have to worry about that. Most news was read. Dad read about 5 newspapers per day. At any rate, the Erie Sunday Times was a meaty paper in the 1980s. It was so big that they had to bring part of it on Wednesday—the comics and all the inserts, including coupons. Those coupons were the reason that people were flocking to get the paper because they more than paid for the 60-cent newspaper if you used one or two coupons.

My Mom used scads of coupons. In fact, she clipped coupons, bought what was on sale, and then decided what to cook. A large paper carrier's sack could hold 15 Sunday papers. I had two sacks and could carry 30. It went pretty fast in weather that permitted the use of a bicycle. The trick was to distribute papers from the left and right side equally, so as to make it easier to balance the bike. Even so, there was a lot of effort in pedaling 30 Sunday papers uphill. Alas, there were months that I could not use my bicycle. Winter in Pennsylvania can be slippery. This is especially true when people consciously decide not to shovel the sidewalk in front of their house. This meant having to reload the canvas newspaper satchels after walking with them empty to the house. It wasn't so bad to zoom a mile by bike to get more papers. It added lots of time by foot. I tried to plan the delivery by walking in loops that started and ended at my house, allowing me to grab another 30 papers. As the route gained subscribers, it was not possible to do this, and I would have to walk some distance with empty bags to get home. Mom would meet me to refill my bags when this happened. Sometimes she even delivered a few papers. I can't imagine how much gasoline it must have cost, but it was cheap then. Her new customer sales resulted in my winning a trip to Europe in 1984. It was sponsored by *Parade Magazine*, and all the winners were paper carriers, for newspapers all over the country. We went to Italy and the former Yugoslavia. I was gone for two weeks. Guess who delivered all my newspapers? Mom, the same person who won the trip, if I am honest. The contest was based on new subscriptions. For every new subscriber, your name went in the hat. Get 10 new customers, and your name went in there 10 times. I gained well over 100 customers, mostly from Mom just gabbing with friends. I am sure there was a lot of luck too. A lot of paper boys and girls worked for Erie at that time.

In 1985 I bought my first beagle for $75. That means I delivered 500 papers to pay for the pup, not counting tips. I bought my first shotgun too. It was a Western Auto brand 20-gauge bolt action. It held two in a magazine and one in the action. It was $60. I paid for it with one dollar bills from the paper route. I used that paper route to buy all sorts of things. Leather dog leashes with French snaps, nice rubber boots, leather collars, subscriptions to beagle magazines, and other things. Like what?

Well, a belt with beagles etched into the leather and a buckle that featured a beagle. Oh, and a jacket that said "Beagle Hunter" on the back. I was forever explaining that I hunted with beagles. I did not hunt beagles. It wasn't the sort of thing that was cool to wear in school, but I did every other chance I got! Especially at the beagle club. At that time, it was not legal to train your dogs in the wild during the summer months. You had to go to a beagle club, where there was an enclosure. The Game Commission granted beagle clubs a permit to have an enclosure and then also granted separate permission to train dogs year-round. In the summer, when I wanted to train dogs, Mom would drive me to the beagle club and leave me there. I took that pup of mine, Duke, and his half littermate (Princess), that my dad purchased. I would be left alone for hours until my mother returned and honked the horn from the enclosure's parking lot.

It seems weird now. I would be gone all day, listening to hound music. I took a couple of jugs of water, a water bowl, a lunch, and a bottle of RC Cola. It seems so different than today.

"Why is he not answering my texts?" my wife, Renee, bellowed the other day.

"Who?" I asked.

"Wes!" she said, referring to her son, my stepson.

"Maybe he didn't get it?"

"Oh yes he did," she said.

Twenty minutes later, he replied to her. For twenty minutes, she was out of communication with him. Oh, he's 22 years old! I was 13 years old and allowed to be dumped off at the club. If something happened, I had to figure it out. Dogs get out of the fence? I better run to get them before they got to the road. Dogs run a fox? Oh boy, that was a test in my running ability. There was no way to call for help. I was beagle crazy and my mom was willing to help me, even if it meant dropping me off in the woods at 7 in the morning and getting me at noon or later. If the dogs got hot, I would give them water, tie them to a tree in the shade, and sit with them for an hour or so before giving them another chase.

Mom and Gram took turns taking me hunting when Dad was working. By law, you had to be 16 to hunt alone. Mom and Gram would hang out while I hunted if Dad was working. Years later she told me, "I didn't mind. People would tell me that you can't pick the friends your kid has. I decided that I should. Bad friends are bad news. None of your friends that hunted were bad kids, so I helped you train dogs all that I could. You couldn't get in trouble in the woods."

"Well," I said, "I had dogs get out of the club and get lost, I got stung by ground hornets, and I had a few scary moments with bears!"

"I told you to stay out of that place during blackberry season! You never told me about bears."

"I knew you wouldn't let me go back. There was also the day that I saw a rattlesnake."

"But at least you weren't in town," she said, "That's where all the real trouble happens."

"I guess so."

"And you loved those dogs so much that you always had a job. That paper route until you were 16 and then other jobs that paid more." It was different then. I routinely spent hours per day alone in the woods. I would go home in the afternoon and my friends were just waking up for the day. Of course, I was only alone because my mom drove me there. And she got me the new customers on the paper route that funded my hobby. Thanks, Mom. I miss you.

LONGBOW LAGOMORPH

One of my fondest memories is from childhood. Every Sunday, my father would take me to the woods with a bolt action .22 long rifle. It had no magazine, you loaded the rounds one at a time. Open sights. We would take a box of shells, and an empty coffee can to an area with an embankment behind it. He would walk the can 30 or more yards away, and then return to stand behind me. I would try to hit it 50 times. I got to where I could do that every Sunday. So, we started getting snuff cans (Copenhagen) from my uncle for a smaller target. Copenhagen had the metal lid. It made a satisfying ping when I hit it. All of this is to say that I am a decent marksman with a rifle. I like to aim.

Anyone can tell you that this is not an asset when you are shooting a shotgun. You don't aim a shotgun. Well, you can, but it doesn't work as well. Trust me, I have come a long way to be a decent shotgunner. Bows? For years, if I hunted archery, it was with a compound bow. I have killed more whitetail buck with a compound bow than any other way. A compound bow has peep sights, you see. You can aim the thing.

A few years ago, I went with a few relatives to the Eastern Traditional Archery Rendezvous or ETAR. It is known worldwide and attracts at least 8,000 people and as many as 10,000 come to shoot traditional bows (no pulleys, no sights, no crossbows). The whole event is here in Pennsylvania, and not real far away from home. There are courses and competitions. Over 100 vendors sell bows, arrows, accessories, and anything else you might need. People swap things like an old-fashioned rendezvous—you can put a limited number of items on a blanket for swap or sale. People camp there all weekend. You visit new friends. Yeah, there was a campground bear that sat 10 feet from our campfire, but that was exciting. The cabin had four beds and a couch. Two guys were outside the cabin in a dome tent. I was in my rooftop tent, on top of the truck. The bear circled my truck after not finding food at the campfire. Was there dog food in my truck cab? Cripes, good chance.

I grabbed my cell phone after the bear circled the truck "Hello?" my nephew answered.

"Is the cabin unlocked?" I asked.

"Of course! There's a friggin' bear out there!"

"I am gonna need you to unlock that door," I whispered into my phone, but a loud whisper."

"Why?"

"Cuz when this bear goes around the other side of the truck for the fourth time, I am sleeping on the floor in there!"

I didn't even use the ladder on my rooftop tent. I jumped, rolled, ignored my aching ankles, and sprinted to the door. The bear pretty much ignored me. I got into the cabin to find the inhabitants of the dome tent already on the floor of the living room. I moved to the small kitchen area and slumbered on the floor. The bear brushed up against a tent with some guys from New Jersey that had a cooler in the tent with them later in the night, we heard the next day. Though I think I heard them scream in my sleep. No one was hurt.

Anyway, shooting a traditional bow is like shooting a shotgun in the sense that it is instinctive. You don't really aim. Well, some do, but the instinctive shooters seem to do the best. They calculate drop, distance, and all the rest in their minds from repeated practice. As you can imagine, this is not easy for me. I can instinctively send hundreds of pellets from my shotgun downrange at a rabbit, all of those pellets expanding as they go, and only one needed to kill a rabbit. And miss. My asset is that my dogs will keep circling the rabbit until I get a shot that I can make, which is usually when I see the rabbit before it sees me!

After watching the ETAR crowd, I decided that I needed to give traditional archery a try—for rabbits. I would trade in hundreds of pellets for one arrow. I decided to shoulder the burden of doing better and bought a cheap recurve there. Golf, in my mind, makes little sense. 3D archery, on the other hand, is fun. You walk around the course, record your score on each target (They have all kinds of critters—deer, bear, moose, elk, beaver, whatever) remove your arrow from the foam animal, and walk to the next target.

Of course, this was when that hunger time stuff was in the movies. Wait, my wife informs me that the movies were called *Hunger Games*. This is important because there were scads of little girls, not old enough to hunt, who were walking around 3D shoots with pink bows. Every single one of them had been shooting since they saw the first movie in that franchise, and every single one of them could shoot very well. They began shooting instinctively and progressed quickly. They gave me pro-tips at the range.

So, I just kept slinging arrows with my recurve. When I was a kid, my dad and his brother would pitch horseshoes. They would pitch from one end to the other, walk down to tabulate score, and then return the horseshoes towards the other stake. First one to 21 would be the winner. Once in a while, if there was a tournament coming, my uncle would pitch shoes alone. He was much more serious about it than my dad. I got two targets—block—from the sporting goods store and decided to set them up like horseshoe pits—so I could shoot to one end, and then gather the arrows and shoot into the other target. Well, in between shooting the arrows, there was a lot of time devoted to finding the ones that missed entirely. Luckily, the fletching of the arrows and the nock are usually visible, even when the rest of the shaft is submerged into the dirt. Did I ever get good? No. But I got to where a 10-yard shot on a small target would not completely embarrass me.

As an avid rabbit hunter, it seems to me that the vast minority of rabbits that have entered my game vest have not been killed within a range of 10 yards. 20-30 yards seems more common with my shotguns. So, while trying to kill a rabbit with a bow, I often find myself watching cottontails amble by at insanely far distances like 20 yards.

"You're lucky I don't have a shotgun," I mumble to myself as it goes past. Heck, even my compound bow, with peep sights, would be easy to use at that range. You can only handle this kind of frustration for so long before you have to take action. This is when I take the small, disassembled .410 SxS shotgun out of my game vest, put it together, hang the bow on a limb, and shoot the rabbit.

I also discovered that a pack of dogs made the hunt more difficult. If I put four dogs behind a rabbit, I was having to shoot at a much faster target than if I took one dog. It isn't as exciting to hear a dog sing solo as it is to have the whole band making music, but a solo hound made my shots easier. When I say easier, what I really mean is that they were near misses. The first dozen near misses on a sprinting bunny are certainly exhilarating. After all, I was accustomed to completely missing the mark! When you hear an arrow rattle off a stand of saplings, you know you missed badly. Or if you see it soar into the multi-floral rose, you can count on never finding that arrow again. Certainly, the near misses were fun. At first. Then, they become depressing. Just under or barely high are the worst. You know that the tiniest change on your end would have made all the difference on the end where the rabbit was. Oh, there are a variety of small game arrow tips that are available, but I seem to shoot better with plain field tips— the same practice tips that I use when shooting at the block targets in the heat of summer when it is too hot to run my dogs. Those field tips tend to bury themselves more than the small game tips. I have ended many archery hunts with no rabbits and thrilled if I found my missing arrow.

Then, I bought a longbow from my nephew. It was made by Wild Horse Creek Bows in Kansas. It just seemed to work better for me than the recurve. You can distinguish a longbow from a recurve by whether the tips of the bow bend toward you when you draw back, or if they curve again (recurve) to bend away from you. I was better with the longbow, at least on target.

So, after a great hunting season for bunnies this year, I decided that I did not need to shoot anymore on the last day of the season. I donned traditional archery clothing—leather and wool—and added my blaze safety orange hat and small game vest. Placed my quiver over my shoulder, and unleashed one dog—Duke—hoping that he could give me a close shot.

Have you ever been facing the wrong way when a rabbit crossed? It crosses behind you? That happened a half dozen times on rabbits within my range, giving me no shot. There were many bunny sightings that were well within shotgun range. I missed a few within archery range. In eight hours, Duke ran 5 rabbits and they all holed or escaped. The sixth rabbit ran past at 25 yards at the end of the first circle and gave no shot. It kept running through the same stand of pines. So, I moved there after several circles. It was quartering at me, streaking through lanes that were created when a coal company planted pine trees in straight rows. The trees were now tall and gave some visibility. I would see the rabbit, then it would pass behind trees, then it would emerge again. As it neared I drew the bow to full draw and the rabbit noticed and paused to turn. It was at 15 yards. I loosed the arrow, and it felt like a near miss—a little high, but the rabbit made a big leap when it turned sideways to me. The field tipped arrow anchored the rabbit to the floor of pine needles, finally success! I hurried to a dirt road before dark, took off my orange, and snapped a pic of the hunt in traditional garb. If you love the chase and don't care if you shoot your limit every time, I highly recommend a bow bunny. Rabbits, by the way, are not rodents, but lagomorphs. I cherish my hunt getting a lagomorph with a longbow.

Black Powder Bunnies

As a youngster, my plan was to grow up and become a mountain man. The idea seemed like a good one. I could hunt and fish all the time, and trap for furs to get my walking around money. I had seen some movies too, so I knew it would be simple as anything to put a pan in the river and get some gold to supplement any major purchases that might be necessary. Log cabins and lean-to shelters seemed easy enough to construct. They built them in the span of one, short, uplifting song in the movies. All the survival books I read from the library made lean-to structures look simple to build. I decided to practice my skills at living like a mountain man as a kid by erecting a structure that I could utilize while camping—why pack a tent, when you have a semi-permanent dwelling. I was so proud that I showed it to my father.

"Hey," he said, "Nice brush pile! But we need you to build them in the beagle club. There is plenty of cover for rabbits here."

"That's not a brush pile," I said.

"It's not?"

"No," I said as a squirrel ran out of it.

"Then what the heck is it?" Only he didn't say heck. He utilized a geographical term of theological origins.

"That's where I can sleep while camping!" I pointed at my shelter

"I thought that I bought you a tent?"

Needless to say, the mountain man lifestyle would take more effort than I had realized. Then I discovered girls. It is tough to get a girl to commit to living in the wilderness. Living on wild game and fish doesn't appeal to most gals. Let alone sleeping in a brush pile. Sure, a nice romantic stroll in the woods is one thing, but sleeping on the ground is another. Whenever my wife, Renee, and I go camping, I take supplies to make sure she is comfortable in the woods. The last time we packed to go for a wilderness getaway the neighbor stopped by with bad news. "It was nice knowing you, Preacher," he said.

"You okay?" I asked him.

"I'll be alright."

"Oh good," I said, "The way you talked I thought we were never going to see each other again."

"Well, we probably won't."

"Man, I am sorry to hear that," I said, "How much time did the doctor give you?"

"What are you talking about?"

"What are you talking about?" I said, "Why else would we never see each other again?"

"Well," he said, "It is obvious that you are moving! You could have told me."

"Oh," I looked at the truck, packed to the gills, "I ain't moving. I am taking Renee camping."

I don't think I could get Renee to live a mountain woman lifestyle. So, I put my dreams on the back burner. Until I got this sweet little muzzleloader. It is a side by side 16-gauge, percussion cap shotgun. Black powder, just like the mountain men. It is perfect for pretending to be in the past. I mean, I would love to hunt and fish for a living. Naturally, it would be great to not be accessible by cell phone 24 hours per day. Then again, antibiotics are nice. Death by diarrhea is no longer a common event in the developed world. I can't begin to tell you how much I miss hot showers when I have been in the field for a week. Solar showers are cute, but they only warm up the water enough to stave off hypothermia long enough for you to build a fire. I like pretending to be in the past. Black powder is the way!

Black powder? That's old school. And fun. You get to carry a powder horn. A possible bag (mountain man purse) is pretty cool too—it can hold your ammo and premeasured powder loads for your gun. I even have traditional wadding for this shotgun—beehive. The traditional wadding comes from a hive that encased my modern electric meter. I accidentally disturbed the pesky wasps by mowing the grass. I got stung—a lot. I vanquished them with bee spray and gathered the remnants of their home to use in my shotgun.

Each barrel takes 70 grains of powder. Then some beehive. Then the same measure of shot—I mix #7 ½ and #6 together, something that doesn't happen in factory loads. Then you have to add more wadding to keep the shot from running out of your barrel. I grabbed that old smoke pole for one of the last hunts of the Pennsylvania rabbit season. It had been a good season, and I had killed a lot of rabbits. I decided to make the day a little more challenging.

We have a flintlock deer season here too. I am a pretty fair marksman with a modern rifle. I can't say the same with a musket. The advantage of the flintlock season (and it has to be a flintlock, not percussion cap) is that if you still have your buck tag, you can put it on a doe if you want. No matter what, the deer has to be close for me. I can't tell you how many times I have fired my rifled muzzleloader at a deer, had a huge cloud of smoke emerge, watched the cloud dissipate, and then saw the deer still eating grass. I can load the gun in less than one minute, but by then the whitetail ambles away, slowly, and either dips over the horizon of a rolling hill or starts eating again, at 200 yards away, which may as well be 1,000 yards. Oh, sometimes there is no cloud of dust because your flint is dull or misaligned and it just goes "click." Then you pull back the hammer and try again. Click. The deer runs.

My muzzleloader shotgun, by contrast, is pretty reliable. It has good range, and unlike the flintlock, the percussion caps go boom every time. I headed afield with traditional gear and traditional clothes. I added a blaze orange vest and hat to be compliant with the law. The first chase was long, and 4 circles later I got a shot. Smoke belched out of the muzzle and hung in the air. It cleared as the dog was approaching. I didn't see the rabbit and figured I had missed. It did not go far, and Duke brought it back on a retrieve. I reloaded as Duke found another bunny. I became transfixed in hound song. His rolling bawl took me back to the brush pile campsite of my childhood.

From there I went back in time before I was born. I thought about dreams of living off the land. A pristine wilderness, with game abounding. I remembered the romantic notion of having a hunting dog in the pioneer days, and always having food ready at hand brought to the gun by the dog.

I do not know how long I lived in my childhood past, but I spent more time in the century before I was born, dreaming of virgin wilderness. I snapped back to the present, and the sun was sinking low. Duke was in full cry. I was not in a wilderness, but on land that had been surface mined for coal just a few decades ago. The rabbit came zooming past me and I held a sustained lead and squeezed. When the smoke cleared, the rabbit was just a foot or two from where it was when I squeezed the trigger.

I decided to set up my modern phone (or is it postmodern) and take some old pictures. Well, pictures of me in old time garb. Me and the dog and the bunnies and the old gun. I was wearing a wool pullover, leather brush pants, and leather boots. I took off the orange vest and the orange hat. I took the GPS handheld, suspended from a lanyard, off my neck, and took the GPS collar off the dog. I intentionally brought a leather leash—not a plastic one in some neon color. I put the cell phone in a tiny tripod and synched it to a Bluetooth remote control button. Sure, it was theater. I killed two bunnies that way. That's all. But it was an homage to our hunting heritage, an acknowledgment of how we used to hunt. All my other rabbits were killed with modern side by side shotguns with modern cartridges. Well, except one rabbit. I managed to shoot one with a longbow the next day. But that is another story, for another time.

It is April now, which means it is field trial season. That means I will be camping at clubhouses in my truck, with a tent. This year, I got a propane water heater and a portable shower stall. Hot showers! Beats sleeping in a brush pile. Maybe my wife will come to a few trials . . .

NOT WISE

There is a lot about this beagle lifestyle that makes me think I am not the smartest person in the world. In fact, it seems that I make all sorts of decisions that would make no sense to most people. My only hope is that you, my readers and fellow beaglers, might be in the same boat that I am. There was a donut shop where my friend Andy and I always stopped to get coffee and food on the way to hunt. I usually stopped there to get coffee on most days, whether I was hunting or not. Andy and I walked in one day and I said, "That guy in the corner is always in here, every time I show up!"

"He probably says the same about you," Andy said.

"What?"

"It's like I said back when I used to hit the bars," Andy said, "How do you know a regular unless you are a regular?"

"Are you saying I have a coffee problem?" I said.

"Admitting it is the first step."

Anyway, I am hoping that you guys are "regulars" like me in this beagle thing and can relate to the stupid things that I do. For instance, do any of you use vacation to hunt rabbits? This is a real touchy subject in my house. I have taken my wife to some pretty nice locations for vacation. She has been to the Poconos. We took the ferry to Nantucket. Cape Cod was a swell little getaway. Oh, it was always offseason. Offseason for tourists. In season for hunting! Fall or winter is always the time to go, and we were there to hunt rabbits.

"All I did was wait for you to get done hunting?" she said one day, on Nantucket.

"Yeah," I said, "But it is the offseason, so no crowds."

"Crowds? It's winter time. It is freezing here!"

There was some relationship tension over that trip. On the other hand, Nantucket is an island with no ground predators and no groundhog holes. You cannot believe how good the rabbit hunting is unless you have done it. It is spectacular. If you take your wife, I will recommend that you take her to a nice restaurant instead of packing cold cuts and bread. I learned that the hard way.

Rod is retired. He and I try to outdo each other for getting to the beagle club in the morning during the hot months of summer. I have a few hunting spots that I avoid in summer due to potential rattlesnake encounters. The beagle club is packed with rabbits and makes for a great place to condition the dogs in the predawn hours of summer. The first person on the scene gets the best running pen. There are 3 other pens. One night, I got called to the hospital to see a church member who was in a car accident. It was 3:30 in the morning by the time I drove home from the hospital, which was 3 hours from my house. I decided to have breakfast and go to the beagle club. I got there at five o'clock in the morning, and Rod was already there! The next day I decided to leave earlier and arrived by 4:30. I was first. I went back the next day at the same time, and Rod was already there—he arrived at 4 a.m.

"You want to take turns?" I asked him.

"Nope," he said, "I wake up to pee several times each night. I don't need an alarm clock. I can get here whenever I want."

"I will just run the other pens," I said.

Veterinary expenses are another matter altogether. Porcupine quills in the mouth, ears cut on barbed wire so bad that stitches were required, and three C-section pregnancies are all on my list of medical bills. One of those C-sections was an anasarca litter (water puppies). When I was 13 years old my first puppy had parvo. Several years ago, I had a dog with Lyme disease that led to kidney failure. There have been several times in my life when I went to the grocery store to get whatever was on sale or being offered as "Buy one get one free" due to veterinary bills. By the way, I am not complaining either. I feel guilty about this at times because I know that there are people who lack health insurance and shop the same way due to personal hospital bills, not veterinary bills. I am aware that my dogs have better health care than some people. My dogs are finicky when it comes to eating medication, and peanut butter is the best trick. I have had several instances when I give a sick dog a pill covered in store brand peanut butter and then make a PB&J sandwich for my supper with the same peanut butter. Then, I give the pack of beagles their supper—expensive dog food.

Standing in the rain is not a behavior typically associated with wisdom. I seem to do it all the time, especially in the summer. My beagles get restless in the house when they do not get to chase rabbits. So, if we get an all-day rain, when they will not overheat in the sweltering July heat, I load up the pooches and head for the briars. Sure, I have a raincoat with a hood and a hat underneath, but I am still standing in the driving rain, and still getting wet. I know it doesn't make sense. If the wind is howling I may not even be able to hear the chase. Rain will pelt my glasses with raindrops and then I can't see much either. Naturally, I do not stay out there if lightning begins, but anything short of an electrical storm means I stand there and brace myself against the elements. A tired house dog is a good house dog.

Time management is another blunder I often make. I know people that can tone the E-collar and get beagles to leave a rabbit chase. I have never taught my dogs to do this because I have always been afraid that I would end up teaching my dogs to never run rabbits! I have had many evenings when I had to shoot a rabbit to end a chase. Worse, it may not be rabbit season, and I have to catch the dogs on a hot line. I might catch one on the first attempt, and put it in the truck. Then two on the next pass, leaving one more to catch. What happens next? I am late for supper. It is bad enough if it is supper at home. It is even worse if I am supposed to take my wife out to eat! This happened to me three Fridays in a row last summer. So, my wife decided to go with me to run the dogs. They couldn't keep a rabbit moving.

"I thought you had trouble catching them?" she said.

"Sometimes I do," I answered.

"They haven't run more than two circles on any rabbit here," she pointed at the dogs as they looked for a rabbit.

"Look at the bright side," I said as I leashed them, "We won't be late for supper."

When we do leave for a vacation, we have to put the dogs in a kennel or find someone to come to the house and take care of them. One kennel that we used promised us that our dogs would be fine with automatic food dispensers.

"I think my dogs will eat all day with those," I said.

"Everybody says that," the kennel owner said, "Trust me, they all eat less."

Three days later we returned from our weekend trip. The beagles had been transformed into bassets. They were massive. We paid a lot of money to get dogs back that were out of shape and heavy. Now, we pay someone to stay in the house. This sounds like a good idea, but part of the process is stocking the refrigerator with food that the house/dog sitter likes. Without failure, the dog sitter does something stupid—like leave food on the counter. Granted, food belongs there in most houses, but my mutts will get it. We will come home after a week to find a dejected house sitter. "Can they open drawers?" she will sob, "I swear that loaf of bread was in a drawer!" The dogs are just as heavy as they got at the kennel with the automatic food dispenser, and we pay a bunch of money to the sitter. And groceries. And a tip. After all, she is distraught over the stress of watching the beasts, hence a tip.

"Did you fall asleep on the couch?" I ask her.

"Yeah," she sobs, "Is that bad?"

"No," I answer, "But the dogs wait for you to do that. They do it to us too. I always walk the house to make sure the food is secure before I sit on the couch. You have to pretend that you are camping in grizzly country."

"How do you live this way??" mascara runs down her tear stained cheeks."

"I am not sure," I shake my head, "We just do the best we can."

"Is that my purse?" the dog sitter looks at a dog in the yard with the contents strewn across the lawn."

"You tell me."

"It is!" she bawls.

"Let me guess," I say as I run out to grab the purse and contents. "You had food in it?"

"Just a granola bar!"

"Sorry about that," I hand her the purse and the contents, "You want this granola wrapper?"

My wife gives her a couple more dollars to cover the cost of replacing the missing granola bar. This is my life, which has completely gone to the dogs. Who would ever live this way? I wouldn't have it any other way. My life is filled with hound music. Even if I am a fool. Happy April Fools' Day.

MAD AS A MARCH HARE

It is the time of year for spring break. Spring break has always been a big deal to college kids. I spent most of my spring breaks working. I would like to say that this was due to a work ethic that is beyond compare, but the reality is that I was not able to afford to go someplace warm. My father had died right after my freshman year, and I was mostly on my own, financially, from that point onward in my life. Don't get me wrong, my mother sent a few dollars, but I was able to go to college because of guaranteed student loans, which I still pay to this day. Students can now access any academic periodical from the comfort of their laptop computer. Back then, such peer-reviewed journals could only be utilized in the library. Sure, you could check them out, but only for two hours at a time. I worked in the library, and part of my job was to photocopy such scholarly articles for graduate students and faculty who had a departmental account that paid for the cost of duplication.

As for my own research, I had to pay ten cents per page to get copies of said articles. When it was finals week, this amounted to $50 or so, in 1995. I would then call my mother. Back then, college kids went weeks without conversations with parents, at times, due to the lack of cell phone service. The cell phone service was poor because there really weren't many cell phones. There were car phones, but only wealthy people had them, and they were huge. Today, you can call a college student on Saturday night of a home football weekend. They won't answer the cell phone, but you can call them. Communication then was all landlines. And people were busy. So, calls home were usually in the evening.

"Mom, can I have a few dollars for photocopies?"

"Are you serious? You bought textbooks?"

"Yeah, but I need to use other sources for my term papers, and I don't want to be stuck in the library, so I want to copy the articles."

"You aren't using this money for pizza and partying, are you?"

"No, I used my money for that."

"O.K.," she said, and I would get a twenty-dollar bill in the mail with a little letter of encouragement. I would make the copies and go home to write on a word processor that had to have each sheet of paper manually inserted before it would hammer the words with real keys like a typewriter. In fact, you could use it as a typewriter if you wanted to do that. I saved money to get it and used it all the way through seminary. It was not as useful as a computer, but was more affordable and still allowed me to write the way I prefer—with coffee and walking around the room, and scattering documents that I need to reference in rows on the floor. If I started printing a 20-page paper at dawn, it took ten minutes and could wake the dead. TAP TAP TAP TAP TAP as the keys hammered the paper. My more affluent roommates, who owned computers, despised my all-night writing sessions during finals week.

I always had at least one job, usually two. The library job was great because my status got to where I was trusted to be able to handle the whole place. It wasn't the main library, but one of the smaller ones, devoted to earth and mineral sciences. Students were the only employees during weekends and evenings. I was trusted to do that alone. Back then a season football ticket was paper, as opposed to swiping the student ID through a scanner as it is done now. I bought one, just to sell it for a profit to some other student who did not submit their form in time to get one. The paper tickets had no listed name. For the most part, I worked all day on Saturday and all afternoon on Sunday, and most evenings.

Spring break saw an exodus of students, and I was left on campus. I could get even more work hours. The library had limited hours during the break, but the graduate students and faculty were hitting the books every day. I worked instead of taking a break. I have the same problem now with getting off work for a spring break, mostly because spring is consumed by lent, a busy time of year in the church. Even so, I try to get away once in a while, though not every year. I can do it if I take a 6-day vacation instead of a full week. In other words, I do not miss Sunday. What have I done with my spring breaks?

I remember in college people went to Cancun, and Fort Lauderdale. I had a few friends that went to some Caribbean island for a week. Ski slopes in the Rocky Mountains were also popular for the kids that could afford it. I have taken a couple of trips north to run hare. My wife grew up in the North Country and has permission to hunt a farm near the Canadian border. That saying "Mad as a March hare" is a real thing. While I have never seen the fighting that occurs between hares for breeding privileges, I certainly have seen similar behavior in cottontails. What I have experienced first-hand is the massive circles that a mad, March hare will take.

"What are you doing?" my wife, Renee, asked me one year, as we stood on snowshoes.

"Waiting for this hare to come back into the country," I said. I was serious too. One year, at Christmas, I accidentally crossed the border without knowing it, until the farmer explained it to me. So, I was nervous on that march day for good reason. Two hours later I heard the dogs coming back. I was out of position. The dogs crossed the border, about 150 yards to the east of me. As Lady and Rebel pushed south I turned to my wife, "Follow me," I said and started walking as fast as I could towards the tracks where the dogs crossed.

"Stay here," I said.

"Why?"

"I am going to follow the hare and dogs' tracks south a few hundred yards and gamble that the hare will come back this same line. If you hear me shoot once or twice I will be shooting at the hare. If you hear me shoot four times, it will mean that the hare passed me and I didn't see it, and I will shoot both barrels into the ground and reload and do it again. That is your sign to cut the dogs off and catch them before they return to Canada. It is getting late."

I set up in a little clearing with my double barrel. The hare came right at me, and I shot. It jumped high, straight-up in the air, so I thought I hit it. I fired the right barrel and missed. It stopped moving but was clearly alive. I reloaded and one shot finished the hare. I heard a shrill, hawk-like bird calling "kaa ta taa kaa." I went to the hare, grabbed it, and got ready to leash the dogs. It was a good four or five minutes until Lady and Rebel appeared, all the while "Kaa ta taa kaa" kept ringing in the air, and I wondered what sort of avian drama was taking place. I put the big running lagomorph in the game vest and headed towards Renee. As I got closer to her, the bird got louder.

"Follow my tracks towards me!" I yelled, not knowing what that bird was doing. She appeared, huffing and seemingly agitated. "Didn't you hear me?"

"No."

"I was yelling?"

"What were you yelling?"

"What does three mean!!" she screamed.

"At a distance, it sounded like kaa ta taa kaa." I said, "It was so high pitched that I thought it was a bird of some kind."

"You're a bird brain chasing mad March hare!" she said, "You said two shots was a hare and 4 was a sign to get the dogs! You fired three times!"

"Oh," I said, "Yeah. I forgot."

"Well, I figured when the dogs stopped barking you had them, but I wasn't sure."

"Sorry."

This was in the days before GPS. Well, it was before I owned GPS anyway since I was a latecomer to the technology. All of my life I had hunted hare, mostly in Pennsylvania, and there were often times of angst as the dogs went missing for quite a long while. All you could do was walk in the direction that you last heard the hounds and wait to see what happened. Running a solo beagle or a brace could often result in a smaller circle. But not always. Sometimes, even with the modern technology, you just don't know.

Four years ago, I was in the same spot with my wife. "Where are they?" she asked.

"Dunno."

"What do you mean you don't know?" she said, "You turned on the tracking collars, right?" Rebel's son and Lady's daughter were running a March hare.

"I lost contact with them at 1.6 miles away," I said.

"Really? How?"

"Signal dropped. Thick cover," I stared at the handheld. It vibrated. "I got them again! 2.1 miles away."

"Is it coming back?"

"I do not know."

"You think it is a hare?"

"I'd say it is a *lievre*," I said.

"So, it is a hare," my wife said. Her ancestors are French-Canadian. "Why did you say it in French? With a terrible accent, I might add."

"Cuz, I think that thing lives in Quebec and was just here looking for love."

"What do we do?"

"It is now at 2.0 miles." I shrugged, as anxious as she was. It took another hour and a half for the dogs to return. I did not even try to shoot the thing, we just caught the dogs and called it a day. My dad called many things by the term "contraption." That is what he called the television, the Atari 2600 game system, and a couple electronic, handheld games that I owned. I like GPS, and can't imagine not using it. It's a good contraption.

"What are you doing?" Renee asked me recently.

"Huh?"

"You are thinking about something," she said, "You are staring off into space."

"Oh," I said, "I was thinking about taking spring break again this year."

"I ain't dealing with that stress again."

"Nah," I said, "I will find a place at least 10 miles from the border."

"You're crazy," she sighed.

"Like a March hare."

Public Land

It is March, and that means back to the running pen for me. I run outside the fence for the entirety of rabbit season, which goes from mid-October until the end of February. I will be honest, when I return to the beagle club after hunting season, I am happy to see the professional bunnies. Those are the rabbits that get chased every day, and they develop a whole basket of tricks for trying to elude the dogs. They are the reason that my dogs can look so good on a rabbit in the "wild." After spending the spring and summer months within the running pen, they are more than ready for the wild cottontails, that tend to run big, squared off circles. And when I do encounter a sneaky cottontail while hunting, it isn't as sneaky as the ones in the club.

I may run in my hunting spots sometimes during the offseason now. Let me explain. I was hunting on state game lands when I encountered a horseback rider. This was in October, at the beginning of the season. "What are you doing here?" she yelled at me.

I looked at the dogs, which were working the brush as I stood on the dirt road looking at the horse, my double barrel shotgun resting on my shoulder, the muzzle pointing behind me. "I'm hunting," I said, wondering how it could not have been obvious.

"Well!" she lowered her voice an octave, perhaps to scare me, or maybe to comfort the horse, "I am not riding a deer!"

"No ma'am," I said, "I am not a biologist, but that clearly is a horse."

"So don't shoot at him thinking it is a deer!"

"I promise you, I would not do that. Even if I were hunting deer, I would not do that."

"When did hunting season start anyway?" she spat her words with disdain.

"Well, dove season started a little while ago, but today is the first day for rabbits."

"I guess I will have to ride on Sundays only! At least you guys can't ruin the woods on Sunday."

"Pardon me?" I squinted. I thought maybe if I looked a little closer I could see her point.

"All the open land and you guys use it all to kill animals." She nudged her horse into a trot as if to let me know she was ending the conversation. I was so taken aback that I was unable to form a rebuttal. I could now, though; and here are a few things that I think are worth knowing.

The Pittman-Robertson Act was signed in 1937 and it puts an excise tax of 11% on guns and ammunition. That money is used to procure land. It also helped grow large populations of wildlife. It is obvious to you and me since we are in the woods all the time, but the parking lot, highway, and the strip mall are the mortal enemy of wildlife, not the hunter. We increasingly live in a time when most people do not have strong opinions about hunting. Some of us do, and we are in a battle of ideas with the anti-hunters. It's the vast majority of people, who have no real strong feelings on the matter, that will be persuaded one way or the other. That will determine the future of our sport.

Now, I love camping. There are times when I just need to be outside. There is no comparable tax on tents and sleeping bags or backpacks. Very often, however, campers and hikers find themselves on land that was procured by the Pittman-Robertson Act. One of the ways that I locate new hunting spots is by looking for rabbit tracks in the snow; however, I will sometimes get a tip from someone in the summer about a spot where they saw rabbits in the previous hunting season. Before I take dogs afield, I will get the mountain bike out for a little ride, since many of the places that I hear about are on game lands owned by the state of Pennsylvania. These roads are gated, and while the gates are open for hunting season, they tend to be closed in the summer. It is not at all uncommon for me to ride these roads in the early hours of July or August before the day gets too hot. I will see other mountain bikers—younger guys that go faster and further than I do. They are enjoying the same roads/trails that I am—no motorized vehicles allowed. But none of our cycling equipment was taxed to buy hunting land and keep it from being developed into a cul-de-sac community.

I had a delightful conversation with a bird watcher. It was on state game lands and he was looking through binoculars and holding a cell phone in the air. "Hello," I said.

"Hi."

"What are you doing with the phone?"

"I am trying to determine the bird that is singing right now. The app on my phone will tell me, and then I will look to see if I can find it."

"Interesting," I said.

"It's a warbler," he looked at the picture on his phone and began scanning the tree line with his binoculars. Myself, I can name a handful of songbird species, but it isn't my passion.

"I hope you find it," I said, getting ready to walk away.

"There it is!" he yelled a whisper, which ended up being the volume of a standard spoken voice. He was looking through a pair of binoculars better than either pair that I owned for deer hunting. Bird apps and binoculars aren't taxed to preserve wildlife either.

I was almost in a yelling match with a guy that had a large mixed breed dog that he was walking in the early weeks of the small game season. He was just walking his dog in the woods when it heard my hounds baying on a rabbit. I heard the ruckus and ran over to see that the big mutt had decided my beagles were disturbing his personal space by chasing a rabbit. I yelled at the dog, and when my trio of beagles resumed the chase, the big dog again ran into my dogs again. I held the big male by the collar. The owner arrived.

"What are you doing to my dog?" he asked.

"Stopping it from getting aggressive with my dogs!" I shouted.

"Well," he sipped from a Starbucks coffee mug, "What do you expect? Your dogs are barking." Needless to say, I had to refrain from getting agitated. That guy, like me, buys dog food, leashes, collars, dog beds, treats, and veterinary care. None of that is taxed to ensure a future for hunting or wildlife.

Don't even get me started on the cost of a hunting license—which I gladly pay—and all the extra stamps. A stamp to hunt archery. A stamp to muzzleloader hunt. There's the migratory game bird stamp because I do shoot a few doves and woodcock. Oh, there was a new pheasant stamp last year—that was $25. So, in addition to the excise tax on guns and ammo (bows and arrows too) our hunting license fees also goes to ensure that we have abundant game and places to hunt.

Public land is a big deal for me. Some of my best hunting spots are on private property, but most of the places I chase rabbits are on public land. I honestly do not mind sharing the woods with photographers, bird watchers, dog walkers, horseback riders and butterfly taggers. I forgot to tell you about the butterfly collector that I chatted with on a piece of land that was prison property but is now hunting land. A guy with a small net was catching butterflies on a warm autumn day. Specifically, monarch butterflies.

"What are you doing?" I asked as Duke was chasing a rabbit.

"Tagging this butterfly," he said.

"Oh yeah?" I thought he was pulling my leg.

"Yes, these swarms of butterflies are headed to Mexico."

"Really?" I said.

"Yep. Most monarch butterflies only live for a few weeks. But the ones born in early fall will go all the way to Mexico and stay there for the winter. In the spring they will breed on the return trip, and it will take a couple generations of monarchs to make it back here."

"I did not know that," I said as he put a sticker on the butterfly wing. It had a number and he would record where he tagged it, so if anyone found the dead butterfly later, it's migratory origins could be known. Duke ran past as I watched him tag a few more butterflies.

"Your dog sounds beautiful," he said. I thanked him and went on to my work of hunting rabbits as he was busy with the monarchs. I am going to work on a way to help explain that we can all use this land, but that I do not want to feel isolated as a hunter. As if I am somehow a lesser person because I shoot rabbits. Bird watchers, mountain bikers, and butterfly taggers can all be allies. Oh, I think I might run in the state game lands a few times this summer too, just to see these other outdoor enthusiasts when I am not carrying a gun and explain to them the beauty of our passion. How it helps support so many other outdoor activities.

Administration

This is no secret, but I despise paperwork. I will tell you how bad it is. When I got married, my wife discovered that I had more money than she thought. Here is how it happened. I rounded up to the nearest dollar on every purchase, even if it was only a penny over. So, if I bought something that cost anywhere from $19.01-$19.99, I wrote it down as a deduction of $20 in my checkbook. If I deposited a check for $112.53 I rounded down in my records to $112. I rounded down on my income and up on my expenses. I did this to be lazy with my math, which is ironic because I was pretty good at math, having had algebra, geometry, trigonometry, and a couple semesters of calculus. But I do not like paperwork.

I did this for so long that there was a $1,000.00 discrepancy between my records and the bank when I got married. I had over a grand more than my checkbook said I did. Nowadays, of course, you just open your smartphone and all of your transactions are right there, and you can verify all of your financial steps. As soon as my wife realized this windfall, my records matched the bank statements. I am still not sure where the money went.

For reasons that are a mystery to me, I never seem to be able to get my driver's license or car registration renewed on time. The paperwork arrives in the mailbox, and I put it up somewhere safe, like on a high shelf or on top of the refrigerator. Reality is that I probably could have thrown the thing on the kitchen table or even on the floor of my truck and found it again, at any given moment. Those envelopes would survive the onslaught of beagles and wet shoes in my truck or the bombardment of coffee and food on the table. But the minute I decided it is sufficiently important to be placed in a safe location? Poof! I do not know what happens. I will find it three years later, wondering why I put it on top of the canned goods on the top shelf of the cabinets.

Inevitably, I find myself standing in line at the DMV to get a new driver's license because mine has expired and I can't find the paperwork. The same thing has happened to me for hunting licenses, and I have routinely forgotten to mail in an application for a doe tag, thus limiting me to a buck only, which I do not get every year. When I got married to my wife, Renee, we had to combine our stuff. She told me that the only thing I brought to the marriage was beagles, guns, and books. She forgot mountain dulcimers. At any rate, she found some boxes of old notebooks from seminary, college and a few from high school even. She was paging through them when she found an aptitude test that was intended to tell you what sort of work you should do for a living in a batch of high school notebooks. Apparently, my proclivity towards administrative work was only in the 32nd percentile. Which means 68% of the population is better at it than me. I'd go so far as to say that the test obviously has a margin of error, and would not be surprised if well over 70% of people are better at it than me. I might read a book per day on hunting, beagles, theology, history or bible study. You know those "terms of agreement" things when you update software or install a new program on your computer? I have never read one of those. I check yes and then click on "continue."

Here is the kicker, I am a field trial secretary at my beagle club. I do all that stuff happily. Heck, I like getting judges and taking entries. I enjoy looking at the entry forms after a trial and seeing what dogs placed. More importantly, I like to see the sire and the dam of the dogs that placed. I have been doing it for enough years that it just seems easy, and I even wade through the AKC website to apply for trials and enter the names of the field trial committee and the judges for each class. I do not know who designed the AKC website, but it is the least user-friendly website that I ever utilize. Thank God they have a couple really great people answering the phone. Navigating their website is like driving in Pittsburgh, PA. Pittsburgh is the closest big city to where I live, and it is clear that the roads were not planned in any modern way. People walked on these paths in pioneer days. Then they put horses on them. Then they paved them and hoped for the best with cars. If you drive there every day, you are okay. Well, maybe okay, they get some fender benders. I do not drive there often, and so it is always confusing. All those swooping downhill curves and twisting upward ascents with intersections at odd angles. You get lost. By contrast, I have been to cities in the Midwest where all the streets are perpendicular and square. The roads are all rectangles and squares. Heck, they are even numbered in order without skipping numbers in between. The streets are orderly and make sense. In my experience, the AKC website is more like driving in Pittsburgh than the Midwest.

So, I ask myself, if mailing in my car registration is too difficult, why do I gleefully do the beagle stuff? I think it is the dogs. I see the value of knowing what hounds I like, and being able to watch them in the field. I get small clipboards for entry forms and large ones for the official paperwork that has to be sent back to AKC. Shoot, I went to the office supply store to get stuff.

"Pastor Bob?" my secretary, Kathy, asked a few years ago as I entered the office supply store in Altoona, PA.

"Hey, how are you?"

"I never thought I would see you here!" Kathy said.

"I need a few things for a field trial," I said, "I like to have a couple good pens for the stuff that needs to be signed. I need a new clipboard too."

"Really?" She said.

"Yep."

"Your desk looks like it goes unused for days at a time in the office."

"Probably weeks," I said. "Well, that's because I don't sit there much. I know we got the desk for free but my knees hit it, and they won't fit underneath."

"I have the paperwork ready for you to sign," she said.

You can't believe how much paperwork there is in The United Methodist Church. All sorts of data that has to be sent to the district office and the bishop's office. Counting attendance. Counting Sunday school. Determining how much money was spent in all these various categories— outreach, property, evangelism, etc. It is stuff that 70% of the world can do better than I can. Kathy signed most of that stuff for me. She was good at it, the signature looked more like mine than my own signature. But I always signed the forms for baptisms, and memberships, and confirmation. The important stuff—the things that dealt with people rather than institutions.

"What are you looking for in this store?" she asked, noticing that I was looking on the shelves.

"I have these forms. There are about a half-dozen of them, but there are four copies of each, one for each class at the trial. There are two male classes and two female classes." I scratched my head.

"Oh," she said, "Get one of these accordion files."

"What?"

She grabbed a binder and opened it. It stretched open and there were six or seven individual slots, each of which could hold a bunch of papers. "That should work," she said.

"Hey," I looked it over, "That will be perfect."

Later that day, Kathy called to remind me that we had a committee meeting at the church. She knew that I might be at the beagle club on a spring evening. It was a good thing she called too because I was just about to load dogs. Kathy passed away from cancer. Trudy is my boss now. In theory, the administrative assistant works for the pastor, but on the ground, it is different. Especially if you scored a 32 in administration. Trudy is the fourth secretary that I have worked under. The good news is that cell phones mean that pastors no longer have to be in an office to be contacted. I run dogs almost every day. In the summer, it is in the wee hours of the morning. In hunting season, it is the last hour or two of daylight. In that time, I can write sermons, prepare bible studies, and be in prayer for the tough situations that people face every single day. Trudy is no-nonsense and by the books. In other words, she will not forge my signature. That's good, it helps me to improve upon my 32nd percentile skills. But she can connect with people really well, and it took her only a year or so to learn how to boss me around and yell at me, which is what I need. Actually, she yells much nicer than Kathy did, which is to say that she can do it in a softer voice. But shame me more. "You still not sure when your last week of vacation will be?" Or she calls me on the phone, "You coming to the meeting tonight? We are all here." But, she covers for me when I forget stuff and is great at keeping committees in a spirit of cooperation. She has a kindness that is infectious, and she can plow through the paperwork to see the real ministry that the administrative material tries to describe. So, I am writing a note to myself now. It will remind me to buy her some flowers for Administrative Assistant's Day. I realize that day isn't until April and it is March now, but I have to give myself some time to plan (32, remember). I think I will place this post-it note reminder up on top of the gun safe so I don't lose it.

Shoes and Gloves

Snow days are one of my favorite events. I suppose it dates back to when I was a kid. The first thing I always did was go door to door to see if anyone would hire me to shovel the sidewalk. Some people would pay me to clean the driveway too. Today, school gets delayed or canceled fairly routinely. It isn't at all uncommon for two-hour delays without snow. If it gets cold they will start school two hours late while it warms from a dangerous -2 degrees Fahrenheit to a balmy +2 degrees. This was unheard of in my youth, way back in the 1900s. Of course, there were bus stops then, unlike today when the bus stops at each house, and we would gather there and play football before school. It was two-hand touch football, and we played on the street. No one ever stopped us from doing that, which seems odd to me now. That was how we kept warm, and as much as I dreaded it, I would wear gloves when it got bitter cold. I found it harder to catch a ball with gloves. My gloves were not like athletic versions players wear now, but rather they were homemade wool gloves from my grandmother.

Typically, I would stay in bed as long as possible on a school morning. Except when it snowed. Then I would get up at five o'clock in the morning and begin praying for the snow to intensify. I would go to the kitchen, where Mom would have the radio playing. After every few songs, the DJ would announce school closings. My school was reluctant to close, and I would sit with eager ears every time they updated the list of closed schools, hoping that it would include my district. School closings are routinely scrolled across television now, but it was local radio back then. Actually, when my stepson was in school, we knew before the television. The school would call the homes of each kid, the phone often ringing before we were awake. Who knows, it may be done by a group text message today.

As soon as the school was officially closed, my sister and I would whoop with joy and I would put on my boots and winter clothes to clean our sidewalks. The front sidewalk and driveway were first, and then I shoveled the backyard walk; which was narrower and led to the dog kennel. Then it was a mad dash to go door to door and see who might hire a kid. The faster you shoveled, the more houses you could do, and the more money you could make. You had to be fast too because there were plenty of other kids doing the same thing. When it came to snow removal, it was a buyer's market.

We all wanted to buy stuff. Only rich kids had an allowance. Kids do not go door to door now. I know, because I have stood at the window thinking, "Isn't there some kid wanting to make money?" Then, I go out and shovel it myself. I have not seen a kid with a shovel in decades. Nowadays, a kid can get money simply by whining. I've seen it, firsthand, with my stepson.

"Mom," he would say, "I just want that one video game. Just please buy it for me. Pleasepleasepleasepleasepleasepleaseprettyplease!!"

"Okay!" my wife, Renee, would eventually cave. She would take him to the store to get the video game or order it online.

"I don't think we should this," I said one day as she gave him ten dollars to buy a used game from a kid at school.

"Well," she answered, "We are not. I am, with my money."

"Okay," I shrugged my shoulders.

"Hey, I am out of cash, can you loan me $20 for lunch and gasoline" Renee then asked.

"I guess," I whipped out my wallet and gave her the money." At least she was buying the mountain of toys for the kid. Or was I? I have never been paid back. Ever.

I used snow day money for all kinds of stuff, mostly for winter. We went through a lot of plastic sleds. A good snow day could make enough money to go to Olmstead's hardware and get a brand-new pair of deerskin gloves and a box of shotgun shells too. After the houses were all shoveled out we would then play outside. Early snow days, in rabbit season, were the best. Before I was sixteen years old, I had to hunt with an adult, by law. If my dad was working day shift I would start calling my relatives to see who would answer the phone and give me a ride to hunt rabbits and then stand there as my legal adult companion.

"Hello?" my Uncle Tom answered. He was retired.

"Hi Uncle Tom, how are you?"

"Bobby?"

"Yep."

"Ah shoot. Is school canceled?"

"Yes, sir."

"Oh," he sighed. "You want to go hunting, I suppose?"

"Yeah."

"Is it cold?"

"Not really," I said, "Big snowflakes."

"I'll be there in an hour."

I have a sneaking suspicion that if caller ID existed then, he would have never answered. He always answered, if he was home and not out for coffee or visiting other retired friends at a restaurant. He would drive his pickup truck to my house and I would load up my two beagles and zoom off to the woods. It was even better if my father had worked 11-7 the night before. He would shovel our walks while I went through the neighborhood, and then we would hunt together.

It seems so long ago. Winter was a fun time them. No one panicked. For a few years now, The Weather Channel has been giving names to snow. In the same way that the National Oceanic and Atmospheric Administration names hurricanes. So, some winter storm named Bill or Joe or something will be hyped and we get 2 inches of snow. The panic seems to be infectious as people run to the grocery store to buy up staples that they should already have. Bread, milk, and eggs. The should add butter and maple syrup because the only thing I can think that you can make with eggs, milk, and bread is French toast.

We have had some winter this year, which has been nice. I saw bugs in swarms throughout hunting season last year, and there was very little snow. This winter has been good. Where I live, om the Allegheny Plateau, we will get lake effect snow and sometimes it can be a bunch. I spend all winter looking for new rabbit spots, just by driving down a road, or walking into the pine trees, and looking for rabbit tracks in the snow. Fresh snow allows me to assess the rabbit population. In recent years, February has proven to be a snowier month than it used to be. This is quite convenient because in recent years we have also been allowed to hunt through the entire month of February.

When the schools cancel, I now show my support and likewise take a snow day. I put a few deboned rabbits into a crockpot with vegetables to make stew. I work from home and stay off the roads, and then, when the afternoon gets to the warmest temperature for the day, I go out and hunt rabbits for the last two hours of daylight. I then come home, put on a pot of coffee, and have some rabbit stew. This winter has been particularly productive, and some cold temperatures in December and January have forced me to learn how to shoot with gloves. It reminded me of not liking to wear gloves to catch a football at the bus stop. Typically, whenever hunting, I would use fingerless gloves. Technically, they were mittens but could be converted to fingerless gloves. While I have been using them in the cold for many years, I now decided not to endure single digits on bare skin. After a few weeks, I managed to get accustomed to the gloves.

One of the things I wanted to buy with sidewalk cleaning money as a kid was a pair of snowshoes to walk in the deep drifts. They are expensive, so I was not only shoveling more but spending less. My dad knew I wanted a pair, and he bought them. I have many miles in those old shoes. I stopped using them as they were old and while maintained pretty well, they still were not in great shape. To save money I bought a cheap pair that had aluminum frames instead of wood, and plastic decking instead of rawhide. They work, but they are loud. Sometimes a rabbit knows where you are and you simply have to relocate. That isn't easy in my cheap snowshoes on crusty snow. Those bunnies hear me moving. But it isn't like I use them every year. Some years I get a few weeks of snowshoeing, especially in the steeper valleys I hunt where there will be significant drifting. Or if I travel north for a late-season hare hunt in New York state. My birthday is only a few days from Valentine's Day, and I got a combined gift for both events early this year—a new pair of snowshoes made from traditional materials. I was ecstatic about the gift, and have been praying for snow even more than I did as a kid.

"That is an expensive gift," I said.

"I am just paying you back for all the borrowed lunch money you gripe about," Renee smiled. I am hoping The Weather Channel gives a February snowstorm the name "Renee" because I am thinking that will produce a good accumulation. My wife knows me well. Happy Valentine's Day.

LOVE

There is always such pressure to be Romantic in February, for Valentine's Day. I have been married long enough that I have sometimes been casual about the whole thing. "Hey," I said one year, "I really love you and here is fifty bucks if you feel like buying yourself something."

On other years, I have been more romantic. I once sent a bunch of roses to her office, so that all the other gals that work there had to see them be delivered. She works in an office that creates an online curriculum for the business college at Penn State, and some of the guys that work there get more computers per year than dates. These men have a sad day or some of them. I understand that the day can be difficult for single people and those who lost spouses. It isn't always a picnic for married folks either. My wife, Renee, and I fight over supper more than any single topic.

"What do you want to eat?"

"I don't care."

"Okay, how about leftovers?"

"Oh no, I am tired of those. Let's freeze them."

"I thought you didn't care?"

"Well, anything else."

"Want to go out for supper?"

"No, I have a meeting at seven o'clock."

"Well, then let's cook something."

"I don't know what we have!"

"We can go to the grocery store."

"That always takes way more time than we think."

"Want to get food delivered?"

"Yeah."

"From where?"

"I don't care."

"Pizza?"

"No, I am sick of pizza."

"Chinese?"

"Sure. From where?"

"Maybe Thai food instead of Chinese?"

"I am not in the mood for spicy stuff."

"They have other things."

This can go on forever, or until I make a peanut butter and jelly sandwich and eat it. Deciding where to go for Valentine's Day dinner is a complete nightmare. Last year, I put rabbits in the crockpot to make fajitas, and let them cook with peppers and onions. When Renee got home from work, she smelled the fajitas and I said, "Why don't we eat dinner at home?" Much to my surprise, she was happy to stay home. That was a good day, which went way better than the year I completely forgot about it. What is worse, is that I hunted until dark. Worse than that, I was in a place with no cell phone signal. When I started driving home my cell phone began to blink and buzz and I pulled over to read all the messages.

It was clear that I was in trouble. I completely forgot. I had missed calls and voicemails into the double digits. The text messages may have numbered 25 or more. I was just starting to listen to the voicemails when the phone battery went kaput. I had no idea how much trouble I was in. I had no charger in my truck. The phone had sat in my cup holder, and the cold air drained the battery while I was enjoying hound music and good shooting. I had a one hour drive to get home. At one point, I thought, "I would be better off slashing two of my tires and calling AAA than wandering into the house with happy dogs and dead rabbits." Alas, the cell phone was useless, I couldn't call AAA! And tires are expensive.

So, I decided I should stop and buy a gift, or at least a card. Gas stations don't really have good cards, mostly they are humorous. So, I got a plain card, and sat there in the cab of my truck and wrote a love letter. I know, how good of a love letter could I possibly write? The answer is, not good. More than that, it took me a long time to compose the thing, which would make me even later getting home.

I stopped and cleaned the rabbits after that too. The last thing I needed was to butcher rabbits at home while

she was mad. The knife would be way to handy for her
to take and use on me. I once was in a hospital waiting
room to see a patient, and the TV was on a show that was
called "Wives with Knives" and I am not making that up.
It was a show about wives who stabbed their husbands. I
never forgot it. I stopped to butcher rabbits on a dirt road.
That added a few extra minutes too. I stopped at another
garage and cleaned my hands because I was going to have
physical contact with Renee when I got home. I wasn't sure
if it would be a hug or if I would be in self-defense mode,
but if my hands smelled like rabbit blood, it wasn't going
to be any easier for me. I thought the whole thing might
be worse than the time I hung out with my buddy Lee on
his birthday and had a big cookout. Did I mention that his
birthday, which he invited me to attend, is on the same day
as my anniversary? Cripes, I thought, maybe the Jehovah
Witness crowd had the right idea in not celebrating days.
I bet whoever decided to make that a rule forgot important
days and got in trouble with his wife. Who knows.

After using the gas station bathroom, I looked for
Valentine candy.

"Hey," I asked the cashier, "You have any Valentine
chocolate?"

"Mister, the grizzled looking lady said, "If you are just
now getting candy for today, you are in trouble."

"Yeah," I sighed.

"I have regular candy bars that are heart-shaped or
have Valentine wrappers on them."

"Really?" I said, "That sounds good. Gimme ten of 'em."

"That'll be $12.50."

"Aren't candy bars fifty cents?" I asked.

"Mister, where did you come from? The year 1985?"

I handed over the money and got home to my wife.

I gave her a bag of candy bars, in a plastic bag.

"What is this?" she looked inside, "Are you saying that I
am a pig and candy makes everything alright?"

"Not at all. Why would you say that?"

"Cuz, there are 10 candy bars in here! Who eats ten
candy bars?"

I gave her the card. Much to my surprise, the handwritten card, with no rhymes and less meter, made her get misty. I saw a tear coalesce and begin to run down her cheek. I knew it was going to be okay. I have to admit, that I was never a great interpreter of women. I had a few dates in high school, but I wasn't a popular guy. I wasn't totally inept at athletics, but I would rather be hunting and fishing than playing team sports, though I did play a little. I was a science and math nerd, and that wasn't exactly the way to become a Romeo. It seems that geeks are now more popular, but that may just be in sitcoms.

I wasn't really able to say that I had an active dating life until I was in college and girls began to realize they wanted a guy that could keep a job and maybe have a career. That made me a slightly better candidate. I was married for a couple years before I realized that when my wife was crying, that was almost always good. The only times it was bad was if someone died. The tears started to run with a little more current as Renee finished reading the card, and I realized it was going to be fine. When her bottom lip started quivering, I knew it was all good. It seems weird to say it, but I thought, "Whew, she's blubbering now!"

I really don't think I wrote anything that required writing skill. But I apologized and I wrote it myself. I do it every year now. Well, I don't always have to write an apology, but I write a card. I do my best to get out of the woods in time for supper now, but it is a low-key event. If I get home a little late it is okay. I still remember the year Renee said, "Those dogs take a lot of time, but there are worse hobbies for a man to have."

We get beagle gifts now too. Like lint rollers to remove dog hair from good clothes. Or, white chocolate, which is not poisonous to dogs. My wife got me a new pair of snowshoes this year. Some years I can use them for late cottontail season if the February snows pile up some snow drifts in the valleys. Some years we go to the Adirondacks to see her family and friends and I can use snowshoes to hunt hare while she is visiting. She got me a good pair of traditional shoes made from wood and rawhide. I have a pair my dad got me, but they have a few decades on them and are a little worn. Really worn, actually. I had been using shoes made from aluminum and plastic in recent years, just to save money because I do not use them every year. I know what the shoes cost that she ordered, and I am going to have to step up my game this year to match the gift. I am thinking of jewelry and a fancy restaurant. I recently tried figuring out what restaurant to call in order to make reservations.

"What's your favorite restaurant?"

"I don't know. I like them all."

"But if you were really hungry, who has the best food?"

"I don't know. You mean comfort food?"

"I guess. Just your favorite. What is it?"

"I like Italian food."

"Really? Which Italian restaurant?"

"Depends. For pasta or salads?"

Good grief.

SCRAPPLE, SAUERKRAUT, AND GROUNDHOGS

There are many oddities about my home state. Well, they seem normal to me, but my wife, an import, thinks that they are weird. For instance, she once said to me, "I can't believe how many choices the grocery stores have for mustard and pretzels."

"It ain't that many, is it?" I said.

"There are a few shelves of mustard, and an aisle of pretzels," she hunched her eyebrows in an arch and waved her hand in the air dismissively, so as to indicate how stupid I was for asking.

"What do you think is a normal amount?" I asked.

"There was only two choices of mustard where I grew up. And a couple brands of pretzels."

Why do we have so many here? The Germans. Growing up German had a few things that maybe are not as common in other parts of the country that do not have as many German immigrants. Like pannhaas. Pannhaas means pan rabbit, but it is really pork. Actually, it is a mushy combination of pig organs and other pork remnants that are boiled off the bones. The minced meat is combined with flour and cornmeal (and spices), formed into loaves, and cooled. You slice these brick shaped loaves into $\frac{1}{4}$ - $\frac{1}{2}$ inch slices and fry it, usually for breakfast. It is delicious, but you can't say that you are eating whatever is left on the pig after it was butchered mixed with cornmeal, so it is called pannhaas, or very often it is called scrapple. You won't find it everywhere, but you should give it a whirl if you do see it.

Sauerkraut is a big deal, especially on New Year's Day, when eating pork and sauerkraut supposedly ensures that you will have prosperity. I have done this every year since I was weaned, and I am still waiting for the prosperity. My own suspicion is that the tradition made you feel better about the fact that you were eating sauerkraut all winter because that is what was available in the old days! Making sauerkraut was a big deal when I was a kid. Everyone had a garden and you chopped the cabbage and shredded it, and layered it in a huge ceramic crock with salt. Cabbage, then salt, then cabbage, then salt—until the crock was full. Cover it up and ignore it for weeks. Scrape off the moldy scum and then can it.

Now, one odd tradition that my people have done has become famous all over the country. It involves thousands of college kids getting drunk outside in the winter. Well, it didn't start that way, but that is what it has turned into. They haul this rodent out of a fake tree stump and then pretend that the awoken critter can tell us how much longer winter will last. It is, of course, Groundhog Day. This happens in Punxsutawney, Pennsylvania. Punxsutawney is a Delaware Indian name that means "town of mosquitoes." I think this may explain why the little bugger always seems to see his shadow, indicating 6 more weeks of winter. If I lived in mosquito town, I would want more winter too.

At any rate, the groundhog is named Phil, and he isn't always in that tree stump. He lives in a glass building attached to the town library with a couple female groundhogs. They haul him outside of town for the big ceremony, and that is where the college kids are getting hammered all night in anticipation of the big event. To me, the great irony is that the town officials who oversee the event are wearing top hats that were traditionally made from beaver pelts. Schools have rivals, and the Punxsutawney Groundhogs are bitter enemies of the Dubois Beavers. Not the fiercest mascots (like a lion or tiger or bear), but this football game makes the radio every year. On Groundhog Day, the town officials are wearing the enemy's mascot on their heads. I don't think this was planned, but rather was the unintentional result of wearing traditional, formal costume.

It would seem the Germans brought this tradition of waking critters to predict the weather. In Europe, they used a hedgehog or badger or something. Pennsylvania happens to be full of groundhogs, which is why I am writing this.

Rabbits will routinely go to groundhog holes and this can be very problematic for the hunter. There are many places that I hunt were upwards of 75% of the rabbits chased never circle. They go straight to a hole. This can be very frustrating. When I was a kid, I lived within walking distance of snowshoe hare, and I would take my dogs there to chase them, often around Groundhog Day. Back then, there was no hunting allowed in February, and a hare was a good chase because they do not go into a hole (well, very rarely).

During the Great Depression, Groundhog was a delicacy. People would get a shovel and dig them out of the ground if that was what it took. Jack, an old timer and a friend of mine, said he loved groundhog meat.

"You're teasing me," I said.

"Nope. I love them."

"Well," I said, "You're in luck. I shoot them in the summer for the farmers who let me hunt their property. And also, my veterinarian gives me a discount for every woodchuck I kill on her horse farm." Groundhog holes hurt farm equipment and break legs on horses.

"Get me a tender one, not a big one."

"Sure."

A groundhog hide is one of the toughest I have ever skinned. I took the "delicacy" to Jack.

"Perfect size," he looked it over, "You didn't get those glands?"

"What?"

"In the front legs. Nasty taste." He produced a pocket knife and eliminated the tiny nobs in the "armpit" of the rodent. "I will barbeque him for supper. You coming to eat some?"

"I don't know," I said, "I'm not sure what to think of all this."

"Come. You have to."

I won't lie, it was good. I mean my expectation was low, but it was good."

"They eat the same thing as a rabbit or a cow," Jack kept saying as we ate it.

I am allowed to hunt until the end of February now. I take full advantage of it too, get out every day for an hour or two until the very end of the season. Some years, especially if Lake Erie doesn't freeze, February or even March become the snowy months. I like to hike on Sundays and look for rabbit tracks. It doesn't seem to matter if I am on old mountaintop removal coal mines that have become clumps of brush and grass, or if I am in a spot that was clear-cut for logs and has early timber growth, there are always tracks leading to groundhog holes. Rabbits will use them, and I suppose it is why I can consistently go back to the same spots and get some shooting.

Myself, I am opposed to jump-shooting rabbits. I know it is popular in some circles, and I would never tell anyone how to hunt with their dogs. I think it is dangerous because you don't know where all the dogs are. One rabbit is not worth risking the life of a dog, which can be very close to the rabbit when the case begins. Also, I prefer to shoot rabbits while damaging as little meat as possible. A rabbit that is running away from me will get hit in the back legs and the back, where most of the meat is located. I am not fond of lead pellets in my food, and I have been known to wait for several long circles to shoot at a rabbit because it kept presenting me with shots that could not be made without hitting a lot of the meat.

The history of Groundhog Day, when it was hedgehogs in the old Country, goes back to the Candlemas celebration. This day was to commemorate Jesus being presented to the Temple, and was On February 2, the same as Groundhog Day. Candles were blessed and taken home for light. Electricity can make us forget how dark winter could be. The light of Christ was the gift that reminded us that we would make it, in the end. The days are getting noticeably longer in February, at least compared to late December. I like to celebrate Groundhog Day with pannhaas. I eat "pan rabbit" for breakfast—well, it is scrapple. Then I go for a hunt and I am a little thankful for the rabbits that run to a hole. That is why I will have rabbits next year, and why the fox and coyote cannot get them all. A couple will usually stay above ground and I will get them. Then I go home and make pannhaas or fried rabbit. I parboil the bunnies to tenderize and then fry them in egg wash and breading. The last days of the hunting season are upon us, and Spring is coming. If you go to Punxsutawney, remember that us rabbit hunters never mind a few extra weeks of winter. Here in Pennsylvania we accept winter for what it is and refuse to panic over a few inches of snow like The Weather Channel does. May you all get enough snow to find a few new hunting spots.

ACHIEVABLE
RESOLUTIONS

Every year my wife will dedicate January to making some sort of New Year resolution. "Well," she mumbled one year on New Year's Eve, "I better finish these cookies tonight because starting tomorrow, I am not eating any more sweets." Sure enough, she did not eat any more candy or dessert. For a week.

"I am going to go to the gym three days per week, starting January 1," she said with confidence one year. It lasted until that February when the temperatures plummeted and getting to the gym before work meant shivering in the car for the drive across town. Then she was dejected.

"You should give yourself a more easily attainable goal," I said.

"What was your resolution?" She asked me.

"To lose weight."

"How much weight?"

"See, I didn't specify. So, one pound lost makes it a reached goal."

"That's cheating," she said.

"Well, what do you call giving up dessert for one week?"

She walked away, but I still say I am on to something here. Lose a few pounds. Work out a little more each year. If I am honest, most of my resolutions have revolved around beagles. Some have been more successful than others. For instance, one year I decided to not run the air conditioner in the summer. The reason for this was that I always found that my hounds were not up to the heat in those July and August field trials. The dogs that live outside were fine. My house mutts sprawl under the window AC unit in my office in the summer. I asked my vet if that could acclimate them to the cooler air and hurt them in the summer.

"Well," she said, "I was at a convention at Cornell, and there was a case I heard about where sled dogs were very overheated because the 40-degree Fahrenheit cabin of the airplane was too hot, compared to the subzero temps they had been accustomed to before being transported."

That encouraged me to just go *au naturel*. By that, I mean no air conditioning, open windows only. By late June my New Year's resolution was busted when it was 89 degrees in the house at night. I had an easy solution, however. The next year, I resolved not to attend field trials in the heat of the summer. That was simple. On another year, I decided that I would run dogs every week of the year. I figured that it would be easy, since I run dogs almost every day, even if it is just for a couple hours at 4 o'clock in the morning during the summer. I also hunt almost every day of rabbit season, and one year I actually did get dogs and gun afield (some days for just one hour) every single day that I could legally hunt. I kept a detailed record every week of the year I planned to run each of the 52 weeks. Then, deer season arrived. Well, technically it was the two weeks of deer season when you can use a rifle.

Pennsylvania gets very serious about deer season. Schools shut down for the opening day, if not the first two days. The season opens on the Monday after Thanksgiving. We had company for Thanksgiving, and they stayed until Monday afternoon.

"We don't have school tomorrow," the little kid said on Sunday night, "It's Thanksgiving break."

"Bless his heart," I said, "He lives in a city that was once a small town and he has no idea that school is closed for deer season."

Anyway, I was not willing to run dogs until I had killed my deer. After I shot my deer, I was certainly not going to train dogs in the wild while the woods were full of guys that only hunt deer for two weeks, and never go again until the next deer season. I could have driven 45 minutes to the beagle club, but I didn't. The end result was that I missed two entire weeks. At the end of the year, I had run beagles on rabbits 298 days out of 365. But I did not run every week.

On another year, I vowed to solo each dog at least three times per month. I am a firm believer that no dog gets better by running with the best dog in the kennel every day. I think dogs that get beat every day learn bad habits like skirting, running mute to get the front, and other faulty behaviors. I thought this would be easy because I do not have a problem soloing dogs. I have friends who cannot stand to run just one dog.

"I tried it," one guy told me, "I was so bored." To be sure, a pack is much more satisfying to the ear. So, my plan was simple, with four dogs that I was conditioning. It was basically a rotation wherein I would solo one day, then brace the next. Then solo, then brace. then run all 4. It went well, until summer. In the summer, I run dogs very early, and the dogs that did not get to go with me were in a state of turmoil. They bounced around the house and howled as I loaded up dogs to go afield. The ruckus woke my wife, who doesn't tend to get up before six o'clock in the morning. I was leaving at 5 a.m. if I was running close to home, and 4 a.m. if I was going to the beagle club.

"You take them all or none." She said to me. This wasn't too much of a problem, as I would just solo one dog and then another. Well, I didn't have time to give each dog two hours of running. I mean, I know that the best hounds in our sport get that kind of work, but it is generally handled by guys that don't work! I don't have 8 hours to solo 4 dogs. I typically have one or two hours to run dogs, either before work or after. I got to feeling bad for the poor dogs that went for the ride but didn't get to chase. So, more often than not, I ran all four. Another broken resolution.

Last year, I vowed to find three new hunting spots. I have a lot of spots, but I like to hunt. I may only shoot one rabbit per day, but I get out a lot. I wanted a good rotation so that when I showed up for the last hour of daylight I could get a good chase and a chance to put a bunny in the vest. I found one new spot pretty easy, and then I was at an impasse. Until I got hauled to town with my wife.

The farmer's market is one of her favorite summer destinations. I basically cart food back to the truck while she browses between stands. She will work her way to all of them and then go back to each for the second time, somehow remembering the price differences and other unknown factors that influence her decisions. When she gets food from one stand, I take it to the truck and give her time to make the next purchase. Sometimes I buy a cookie or ice cream. Then it hit me. I bet some of these guys have rabbits that they wish were gone.

"You have guys try to hunt your farm?" I asked.

"Yeah," the guy shook his head to tell me I was not welcome, "I have too many."

"Cool," I said, "I understand. I just know some farmers would like to get rid of the rabbits."

"Rabbits?" the guy waved me back. "My relatives and friends are all over the farm in deer season. You come kill rabbits anytime you want."

I had the same, or similar, conversation with a few farmers and got access to some new spots. Granted, some of the farms were too small, or too close to busy roads for my liking, but adding a few new hunting spots to my rotation made for good chases all season long. It definitely helps if you are giving the farmer some money for vegetables every week.

"Don't we have lettuce in our garden?" I asked my wife, frustrated a few years ago.

"Yes," she sighed, "But not this kind of lettuce."

Heck, nowadays I can't wait to go to the farmer's market. The best thing is that once in a while there is a new vendor who may have nuisance rabbits just waiting to make the way into my frying pan in November.

"Are you ready to go buy overpriced heirloom tomatoes?!" I will yell up the stairs as my wife is deciding if she wants to wear sandals or shoes to buy produce in a parking lot.

"I am almost ready!"

"Well, hurry up! I want to buy weird shaped squash from that new guy. I have a hunch his farm has hedgerows!"

See, that is an easy resolution. Well, I am off to the woods to fulfill my resolution for this year. I vowed to take at least one kid hunting each year, and one retired guy that can't keep dogs of his own anymore. It isn't a difficult resolution, and it is definitely an attainable vow. One is about honoring the guys that paved the way. The other is about making sure these youngsters replace us and our sport continues. Happy New Year!

LIES

Have you ever considered the process of lying? It starts young. I have watched kids tell bold lies. "Did you eat candy after I told you not to eat any before supper?"

"Nope," the kid shook his chocolate stained face. Nobody taught the kid to lie, they just do it. Sometimes, we just accept a lie. I have hunting partners that consistently lie about how many deer they see, how many rabbits they kill, and how well their beagles chase. I routinely lie to my wife, Renee, about her wardrobe.

"Do you like this shirt or the red one?" she asked.

"The red one," I lied. I started lying about these questions because the truth was interpreted as a lie. I used to say, "I don't care, they both look fine."

She obviously did not like that answer. It then took another hour for her to get ready to leave. Sometimes I think we tolerate human lies more than canine. I have seen people go crazy over a dog with too much mouth, or one that ghost trails (lays a line) or dog tracks. Then they get told a real whopper by their kid, "I guess my cell phone turned itself off somehow and I didn't hear you calling." The guy believes it, despite the fact that the kid is constantly looking at his phone and texting.

One of the great lies that we accept is the date of Christmas. Let's be honest, the Bible doesn't say, and we have no idea when it happened. Some experts speculate it may have been in the spring because the shepherds were in the field with the flocks. You can find other experts that say winter, and hence confirm the December 25 date. Christmas on Dec 25 started in the 4th century, and at the time December 25 was the biggest party day around. In the Roman calendar, it was also the winter solstice or the shortest day of the year in the northern hemisphere. The big party celebrated the birth of Mithras, a pagan sun god and was a very popular holiday. So, the church decided that December 25 was the birth of Jesus. They basically claimed the day and stole it. Christianized it.

I first wondered about this date issue as a kid, because here in Pennsylvania, as well as other places, there are large numbers of Orthodox churches and some of them celebrate Christmas on January 7th, which is this month. As an adult, I began to see an advantage of being an Orthodox Christian when it comes to buying presents. The deals that emerge on December 26th can make Black Friday and Cyber Monday look like puny discounts. Orthodox friends told me that they wait to buy presents after December 25th. They spend way less money that way.

That prompted me to exchange gifts with my wife like the song. You know, the 12 Days of Christmas. Those 12 days run from December 25th until January 5th. I give her 12 gifts. Granted, most of them are not very expensive, but I always get her at least one nice gift, sometimes several. I purchase almost all of them after Christmas. Well, after western Christmas but before Orthodox Christmas. Whatever else we can say about the holidays; we must admit that Christmas has become very commercialized. I know people who have overspent for Christmas and acquired a credit card debt that took an entire year to pay. One of the things that we like to do in our house is celebrating Epiphany (January 6th), a lesser known holiday that is actually older than Christmas. It has roots in the Eastern Church. It is a day that celebrates the manifestation of divinity through the Christ child and is often associated with the Wise Men. It happens to be on a Saturday this year, and we often serve a wild game dinner and invite friends.

We have a few friends who eat game but do not hunt. Or they don't hunt well. Other perennial guests are very accomplished hunters. We usually serve venison steak. I was given some bear meat that will be present this year. I still have a couple pheasants in the freezer. Oh, and there is always rabbit. The annual feast began in an attempt to make room in the freezer. This was when we first got married and only had the small freezer above the refrigerator.

"We have a problem," Renee said.

"What?"

"Too much meat in the freezer."

"What?" I said in disbelief, "There is a whole deer in there minus the bones. A few rabbits. A couple grouse. What is the problem?"

"Every time I buy ice cream I have to eat the whole pint. There is no room to put it."

It is worth noting that my wife likes Ben & Jerry's ice cream and all the unique flavors. "You didn't seem upset when you scraped the empty cardboard container clean last night," I said. Have you ever said something that you regret right away? I tried to think of something to make it better, "Ice cream doesn't seem to make you gain weight like it does to me, so what is the big deal?" I said.

"Stop it. There is no room for anything in there. No ice cube trays even."

"So cook it all," I suggested.

"Yeah," she answered, "How much can you eat."

"Let's have a party," I suggested.

"For what?"

I looked at the calendar and said, "Next week is Epiphany. Let's have an Epiphany party and invite friends." And so, it began.

The day always starts with a rabbit hunt. I go afield while Renee starts cooking the wild game. Oftentimes, our invited company brings dessert or sides. It turns into a prolonged feast that includes dinner (maybe you call it lunch) and supper (maybe you call it dinner). We observe the blessings of the Christ child and the nativity and basically have a lazy afternoon. We listen to Christmas music. We tell hunting stories. We have an evening treat hunt for the pooches, where we put the beagles in the basement then hide small dog treats all over the house, to see what dog exhibits the best nose.

At some point, after the company has gone, I will break out my mountain dulcimer and play some Christmas carols. Sometimes my wife will sing. We sit by the fireplace and I will clean whatever shotgun I used earlier in the day. It is now a big tradition. That being said, it hasn't been going on all that long. The Christmas music, the Christmas carols and all the rest are part of the big day. Did I mention the cookies? My wife is in a cookie exchange program wherein she bakes cookies and trades them with her friends. Every year they try to impress each other with new recipes. Then, they exchange recipes that are wanted. Epiphany usually ends with me eating cookies like Santa Claus and napping on the couch with a beagle or four on my legs.

It has the wholesome appearance of a religious observance, and it is. Now. But to be honest, it started as a way to make room in the freezer after hunting season, especially after deer season. We had no ice cream, no ice cubes, and no frozen juice concentrate. Frozen pizzas, a favorite of my stepson when he was still a kid and living at home, would not fit in there. Sometimes we would force food in there and slam the freezer closed, and then when you opened the door an avalanche of frozen meat would tumble to the linoleum.

Even so, Epiphany, an ancient but somewhat obscure holiday, has become vitally important for us. It is about the ramifications of faith and all that Jesus did. We sing sacred songs. It is completely void of the profit-making that can tend to characterize Christmas and escapes all the secular trappings. I think I may look forward to it more than I do Christmas.

So, is it a lie? The December 25th birthday, I mean. No one knows the date. That day has as much of a chance of being accurate as the other 364 days including January 7th. Conflict is inevitable, and I remember a lecture from a former professor about the civil war in the Balkans, within the former Yugoslavia. He said that the violence was between the Christians and the Muslims and also between the Catholic and the Orthodox Christians. Apparently, he explained, armed gunmen would enter a house at night and order the inhabitants to make the sign of the cross. Western tradition is head, chest, left shoulder, right shoulder. Orthodox is head to chest to right shoulder to the left shoulder. The difference is left to right versus right to left.

So, people at gunpoint would go head to chest. The next move determined your life or death. Are the assailants advocates of left to right or right to left? There was great violence here, based on truth—are you right to left or left to right. I am a Protestant, but I can point to much violence that Protestants have done as well. So often the truth, or the desire for it, has been behind great violence. I certainly don't want to say that this violence is okay or sanctioned or Godly. It certainly does not represent the views of most people of faith.

One of my best spots to hunt rabbits is a Christmas tree farm. "You can hunt here anytime, just not between Thanksgiving and Orthodox Christmas," the owner told me. So, I never go until after January 7th. No one getting a tree there fights about the date of Christmas or the differences in beliefs. I think about that while I am in that massive tree farm, listening to beagles sing in large looping circles. Orthodox Christmas marks the beginning of my hunting in a great spot that has been untouched all season. Lies about what I start a wild game dinner are now infused with meaning and truth. Speculation about when Christ was born provide joy on two different dates. Zealousness for truth can be very violent. Can lies be okay? The days are getting longer and I am excited about the January and February hunting season. I hope you have a wonderful epiphany on January 6th. I also hope you had a great Christmas or will have a great Christmas, depending on the day you observe it.

I have to go. My wife is asking my opinion on what rabbit recipes to cook for Epiphany. I really want the rabbit bratwurst, but that is a labor-intensive recipe. I will probably lie and ask for rabbit stew to make less work. And here we go with untruth again . . .

Harey Situations

I grew up in northwestern Pennsylvania, which is unique insofar as it is a place where you can routinely chase cottontail and snowshoe hare. As a kid, I could walk my dogs to places that held both, though not typically in the same locations. The hare were found in the hilltop hemlocks, and the cottontails populated the briars. South of where I lived, it was all cottontails. Southern New York state had places which also held both species. Many states in the northeast are primarily hare hunting spots. Perhaps you are planning a hare hunting trip between now and the end of the winter season to a northern state. Moreover, you may have gift cards from Christmas, and you can take advantage of the post-Christmas specials to get the equipment that would make for a better hunt. While I do not claim to be the best hunter, I have had success on both species, and here are my recommendations for ways to spend those gift cards to maximize your hare hunting success as you chase the white ghosts of winter through the evergreens.

Wool. I have a beagle that fetches dead rabbits, which is a real luxury. For the most part, dogs will eat the bunny. So, I routinely find myself in the briars, as do you, when hunting cottontails—just to get the dead rabbit before the dogs arrive. While I know people that insist that they do not need briar proof clothes because they send the dogs into the brush, I also know that waiting for a cottontail to run into an open field for a clear shot is not the most productive way to kill rabbits. I get into some briars to get good shots. My go-to fabric for these hunts is cotton duck. It stops thorns. If you have ever been in the snow, however, you no doubt have found that cotton is not the ideal material. It gets wet, it stays wet, even the wax coated cotton that is more weather resistant. If I wear waxed cotton duck, it is over wool. Wool keeps you warm, even when you get wet, and it does so even when you sweat. I wear wool pants and layered wool shirts. I am a fan of wool base layers as well. I wear wool socks afield all year, even in the summer. Get a thin pair of wool socks and compare the results versus cotton when you train dogs on a wet summer morning in rubber boots.

The Nylon faced briar clothes are even more problematic for hunting hare. They are "swishy" in that they make a swishing noise as you walk. It isn't always a problem when hunting cottontail, because the rabbits do not run as far as a hare, and if I do have to relocate to shoot a bunny, it isn't a far walk. If your pack get on a March hare in Maine, the circle will go out over a mile fairly routinely. It may stay out there and then come back. I relocate for hare more frequently than I do for cottontail. For the most part, I can see a cottontail on the second, third, or fourth circle without having to move. I can't say the same with hare. That nylon faced stuff is so loud in the dense hemlocks, that everything can hear you moving. It makes it much more difficult to get to a spot in front of the quarry without your location being discovered. Thick wool can also shed briars, but briars are not the common vegetation when hunting hare.

Compass. We all run GPS collars, and you can easily mark the location of your truck. Quite honestly, I do not often look at my magnetic compass when I am in the field anymore. That being said, batteries can drain, and satellite connections can be problematic. I always carry a compass for hare, especially when I have driven to New Hampshire, Vermont, Maine, or someplace that I do not typically hunt. Good hare cover can take the form of densely packed cedar trees that are so close to one another that you can barely fit between them. Some of these "blocks" of trees are massive. You could go miles before hitting a dirt road, and that dirt road may not see anything but logging trucks, and the next one might come by next week. When you are in the middle of a maze of cedar trees, all planted at the same time after a clear-cut by the paper mill that owns the land, and all those trees are the same size—well, it can be tough to remember where in the world you came from. Thankfully, the GPS systems we use to track our dogs can tell us this information. Oh, speaking of GPS...

Antennas. Get the long-range antennas for your handheld that tracks your dogs. It isn't a bad idea to get the roof mounted antenna as well, just in case you have to drive to get to the dogs if they have run a couple miles away on a hare. Last year I was in New Hampshire and my dogs went over a hill and at .5 miles I lost communication with the collars. I have no idea how much further they went.

"I better go to them," I said.

"You don't want to go over that hill," Kris, my hunting host said.

"Why?"

"It's steep, rocky, and too thick to walk anywhere," he said, "The hare should come back, if not we will drive around to them." The hare did come back, two hours later, and was shot. For almost all of that time, I was out of GPS connection. I was a little nervous, but it was exactly like hunting them in my youth when there were no tracking collars. Had it become necessary to drive over the next ridge, I would have utilized a roof mounted antenna that could extend my effective tracking range.

Batteries. I use SportDog, and I carry an extra, fully charged battery for the handheld just in case. My buddy had a Garmin, and it used regular batteries. He kept extras in his hunting vest, just in case. Batteries are also important to keep for the next item that I always like to have when hunting hare with other people.

Radios. A walkie-talkie is invaluable when you are separated by long distances from other hunters. Get a little twisted in the big trees? "Hey, can you whoop?" is something I say over the radio. When I hear the guy yell "Whoop!" I then move in that direction. Hunters can also use the radios to communicate things that you can't necessarily yell, due to the large distances that can separate hunters.

"I got your old dog with me."

"Rover is limping."

"there is a big swamp here that we cannot get through."
"Let's work the dogs back towards the truck."

Don't get me wrong, I am not a big fan of constant chatter on the radios, but when you need them, you really need them. Several years ago, we went to Maine and accidentally met a guy from Pennsylvania at the same hunting outfitter. He had dogs and two friends that did not have dogs. They invited themselves to hunt with us, as they had no success the year before. The dogless friends had no GPS, no compass, and initially no radios. We spent half the time making sure that those guys did not get lost. They were constantly yelling, or worse, following those of us that did have dogs, and hence GPS. They routinely walked in front of us to shoot the hare or try to shoot it. Often they simply made so much noise that the hare turned. They bought radios after nearly getting lost.

Heel. In Vermont, I caught my dogs and a large swamp separated me from the truck. It was getting dark, and I was done hunting. I tried to lead the dogs on leash. There are many places where you cannot do this. As the trees are so numerous and close. The dogs go one way around the tree, you go the other, the leashes get tangled. I had to take them off leash and then make sure that they did not chase another hare, not the easiest thing to do since dusk is a great time for the big jumping critters to get active. I had recently decided to train my dogs to stay close using the tone functionality of my tracking/training collar. When the dogs hear the beep, they know to come to me. I taught them this skill because I had the same trouble with leashes and trees the previous year, and my friend, Mike Leaman, led his dogs out of the thick forest with no leashes. I was immensely jealous and spent the summer ensuring my dogs would do the same. I got my dogs to a dirt road and leashed them. I waited for help.

Snowshoes. I have utilized snowshoes for hare since 1986. My first pair were traditional wood. I have also owned aluminum framed snowshoes with plastic. I must say, the traditional wood is much quieter on crusty snow when moving. Loud snowshoes can be more detrimental than swishy clothing. Modern materials are a little more durable and require less maintenance. Snowshoes are not hard to use, even on your first try. It isn't like skiing. I can cross-country ski a little. Downhill skiing is getting easy for me too, except when it comes to stopping. Stopping, incidentally, is a key part of downhill skiing. I just sit down, which is not the proper technique. Snowshoes are easy and can be used for other hunting. It hasn't been too many years since I have used my snowshoes for cottontails in the second season. The price can vary, and if you are going on a one-time trip to the northlands to shoot a snow-white hare for the taxidermist, then I would not go for the most expensive pair. Even the cheapest shoes are quiet and effective on powdery snow.

Fire. Getting stuck in the big woods overnight is scary. It is even scarier without fire. I carry fire starter, a butane lighter, matches, and a candle. If I have to spend the night, I want to be warm and have the psychological advantage of a fire. A good sharp hatchet or wire saw is good to have as well.

Well, if you will excuse me, I have to give my wife her remaining presents. You see, another thing about this part of Pennsylvania, besides having hare and cottontail, is that we have Orthodox churches as well. They celebrate Christmas on January 7th. I was talking to a hunting buddy that was raised Orthodox, and he said it works out great for presents.

"Why bother with Black Friday and Cyber Monday?" he said, "The price really drops after western Christmas on December 25th."

That made me revive the tradition of the 12 Days of Christmas. I give my wife presents for 12 days in a row, usually small ones. Candy might be one. A new pair of gloves. A book. I usually get a big deal on something around December 28 or 29. I got a big discount on a necklace that I hope gets me cleared for a hunt up north, on the Quebec border, later this month. Happy Hunting, and Happy New Year.

CAPONS

I was recently in one of those fancy grocery stores. You know the kind, they are designed for the person that has lots of time, and they are wanting to make grocery shopping an experience. I was there for the free Wi-Fi in the café, and the cheap coffee refills. When I was done working and full of coffee, I packed my laptop and decided to grab a few items. I should note, that I typically only shop in one grocery store, the one closest to our house, because I know where everything can be found in that store. But they don't have Wi-Fi. Or freshly brewed coffee to drink and a place to drink it.

I was on my third lap around the store, looking for regular sliced bread, instead of the "artisanal" bread that sold for more money per loaf than many people make per hour. Then I saw it. A capon. A capon, if you are unfamiliar, is akin to a rooster in the same way that a steer is like a bull. Snip snip. My grandmother lived through The Great Depression, and at that time when people hatched eggs for meat chickens, they would castrate roosters. This cut down on barnyard violence (roosters are mean, especially to each other) and it also made the birds get bigger and fatter.

My Gram always preferred capon over turkey. Since she always came to our house for Thanksgiving, my mother would have to cook a capon as well as a turkey. Nowadays, chickens are making a comeback. I see free range chickens all over the place. They are in neighborhoods, running around downtown areas, and some people keep them in the house, which seems weird to me. Last summer, my wife, Renee, took me to a farmer's market where she would shop and I would carry the stuff she purchased. She gets a little crazed in farmer's markets, so she takes a cash budget with her, and when it is gone, then we are done shopping. It isn't all that different from gambling fanatics or alcoholics—when the allotted funds are used up, it is time to go home.

"This is organic, free range, antibiotic-free chicken," the farmer said.

"Ooh," Renee said to the guy then turned to me, "You want to grill chicken tonight?"

"I guess," I squinted but saw no price listed for this poultry."

"I'll take one!" my wife said."

"That'll be $20." He extended his hand and my wife paid the guy. He handed her a small bag. We started walking to the next farmer's stand.

"Umm," I whispered, "Did you get a raise?"

"No, Why?"

"I didn't realize we had come so far in this world as to be the kind of folks that eat $20 chickens! I've shot grouse bigger than this thing."

"Honey," she put her hands on her hips, "Of course it is smaller. It is free range."

"Judging by the weight in this bag," I lifted it up in the air, "That thing spent more time running from fox and coyote than eating. That is free range."

When I was a kid, living in rural Pennsylvania, you did not see capons on too many farms. So, they were a little hard to find. Some butcher shops and grocery stores would carry them once in a while. As Thanksgiving approached, we would look for one, and some store would have a couple. There were a couple years that they did not.

"Claude," I said as I arrived at his farm to hunt rabbits, "You had a capon a few years ago, got any more?" I walked up to him and sighed. It was all uphill from my house to his.

"Nah." he was working on something in the barn.

"Where is the bull?" I asked as I let the dog loose from the lead.

"Far pasture," he said, "I knew you were coming." The bull had put the run on me several times over the years. The first time I saw a rodeo clown I was impressed by how close they got to bull to save the cowboy. I was an expert at diving over electrified barbed wire fences, sustaining minor shocks and moderate cuts.

I hunted for the morning and got a few rabbits for rabbit stew, one of my favorite Thanksgiving meals. I started walking for home.

"How bad does she want that capon?"

"Oh man," I said, "I have been to every store in the county!"

"I got the meanest rooster in the world. We can clean it here, leave the feathers on it, how is she going to know it was a mean rooster and not a calm capon, other than the size?"

"Sounds good to me!" I tied the dog to a tree and in a short time I was on the way home with three rabbits in one side of my game vest, and the tail feathers of a rooster sticking out the other side." Gram was pretty ecstatic. "Thank you!" she smiled, "Even if it is a little small."

"Well," I said, "I got it for free, I hope it is okay that the farmer didn't pluck it?"

"Free? Wow!"

Of course, the feathers were on it so she knew it was a rooster, or what she thought was a capon. But I knew the fact that it was free would really get her happy. She was sure that The Great Depression was coming back for round two to wipe us all out, the way influenza mutates and takes vengeance.

This was my first Thanksgiving since Dad died, and I was a little puzzled about what to do on Thanksgiving. I was down to one dog too. In the wake of my father's death, Mom sold our dogs, except my favorite one. She sold his truck too. It didn't make sense to me then. Dad died at 64 years of age but had been too weak from cancer to have worked the last couple months. Mom had no work history but did get a job as a cashier. She was in her 40s and needed to make her own way. It makes sense now, especially since I was away at school and unable to take care of the dogs. At any rate, Dad and I always hunted on Thanksgiving, just to avoid the arguments in the kitchen between my mom and Gram.

"Your mother and her mother cannot agree on anything," he would say to me when he was living.

I was trying to determine where to hunt without a vehicle. I thought that perhaps I would just do homework since I was in my second year of college. I pondered this conundrum all day on Wednesday, Thanksgiving Eve when the phone rang. "Are you hunting tomorrow?" the voice said.

"Who is this?" I asked. This was before caller ID

"Tom," said my dad's older brother.

"Oh, okay. I don't know yet."

"Well, you can take my truck if you want. I know you and your dad loved to go."

"Sounds good to me!"

I felt bad for my mom because Tom would sit in the kitchen and talk her ear off. I felt bad for Tom because I don't think he ever spent that much time with my Gram.

I can't remember much about the hunt. I know I went to a favorite spot that my dad liked for the long chases. I remember the big chases, and how I would sit on a log and listen, the way Dad always did. I shot one rabbit because the point of Thanksgiving hunting was to hear dogs and avoid the cluttered and busy kitchen, shooting a rabbit was a bonus. I returned to the house after noon.

"How was your hunt?" Tom asked.

"It was really good," I said, "How was your morning?"

"I haven't peeled that many potatoes since I was in the army," Tom said, "Oh, is Myrtle (that was my grandmother's name) cooking a chicken?"

"Capon."

"What?"

"Don't ask. And thanks for letting me use the truck."

"Sir?" a voice said to me.

"What?" I answered.

"You've been staring in that cooler for quite a while. Do you need assistance?"

"Oh," I said, "No, I am fine." I was still staring at the capon. They are all gone now. Mom, Gram, Tom, Claude.

"Well, many people ask us what a capon is, and how to cook it."

"Oh," I said, "I know how to cook it. Say, I do need some help. Do you know where the plain old sliced bread can be found? I've been looking for it." She pointed me in the right direction.

Have a good Thanksgiving, everyone. I will be afield. My wife and her mother do not get along any better than my mom and Gram did, at least not at cooking. I hope we aren't eating organic, free-range turkey, that might run $150.

CAMPING

When I was a kid, sled riding was a big part of the winter fun, especially over Christmas break. I can't speak for your neighborhood, but in this modern era, it is not at all uncommon to see towns around Pennsylvania where many homes have a $10,000 (or more expensive) ATV sitting in a yard next to the $500 family car. There were no four-wheelers in my childhood, though 3 wheelers were becoming popular. Plenty of people kept snowmobiles. So, we walked up long, steep, dirt logging roads with plastic sleds towed behind us. You might walk for a half-hour to get a ride that lasted a mere few minutes.

Rides early in the year might be bumpy. With a few rocks or downed limbs poking at the underside of your sled. As the snow deepened, the ride smoothed. Naturally, we went down the hill on our stomachs, since this allowed you to utilize your arms to turn. You see, the logging roads were not straight up the hill, as that would be too steep. So, the roads were cut so that they snaked up the hill, following ridgelines in places, cutting through a natural bench in the land in other spots. If you jumped on the sled face down you could pull at the earth with your hands to overcome inertia, and slowly redirect your path to make the impending curve. How long did we go sledding? It depended on how many times you were willing to walk up the hill for the thrill of the descent. Years ago, there was a television show called "Wide World of Sports" on ABC and it began by saying that it narrated "the thrill of victory and the agony of defeat." When the guy actually said "agony of defeat" there was a ski jumper that tumbled off the end of the jump. I always felt bad for that guy. Vinko Bogataj is his name. I know that now, thanks to the internet. I had no idea who he was when I was a kid. I just knew he was famous for a bad day. I have seen kids take wilder rides off the end of a logging road. I myself almost plummeted down a steep slope. Thankfully, upon exiting the established road I managed to slam my ribs into a large oak tree, thus stopping my acceleration and knocking the wind out of me.

"You okay?" Bill asked me.

"Yeah," I said, "I just can't breathe."

"Oh good," Bill said, "you might have been hurt bad."

"Tell me about it!" I said. "Well, at least I am closer to the top..." and I limped up the hill for another daredevil downhill. You might be asking yourselves, "Where were your parents while all this was going on?" That's a really good question. This was before cell phones. We would go missing for hours at a time. It was also before parents took a real active role in scheduling the free time of kids. Don't get me wrong, I got in trouble when I got home.

"What's wrong with you?" my dad asked.

"Hit a tree sledding," I pulled up my shirt to reveal a massive green blob of a bruise."

"Where were you sledding?

"From the top of the old mill reservoir road down to the detour road," I hung my head.

"That's a long and steep ride," he said, "What's the matter with you?"

"I don't know,"

"Well," he shook his head, "Next time start your turn faster. You could have been hurt bad going off the side of that road."

One year Tim did go all the way to the bottom, somehow missing all the trees. His sled was stuck in the snow, perpendicular. Tim was in what I would later learn is a state of shock. At that age, however, I just presumed he had a mystical experience in nearly meeting the divine. He had experienced massive velocity and near misses in such massive proportions and succession, that he was almost transformed from the experience. He had a glow about him, though that may have been a combination of wind burn and a redness from plowing his face into the side of the nearly perpendicular slope when he left the road. It made Vinko's roll into fame look quite tame. Sledding is almost safe today. There is plenty of adult supervision. Kids don't walk anywhere. Many times, a parent will operate an ATV to haul the kids to the top of the hill. Safer yet, the local ski slope, where I live, offers inner tubes for kids to ride down a gentle slope in well-maintained lanes to ensure that the sleds (well, inner tubes) do not make any contact. The black diamond ski slope looks more like the sled rides of my childhood.

There is a pulley system to tow the tubes to the top of the hill while the kids sit in them, so there is no long walk. The bottom of the small slope has a wall of hay bales to prevent a kid from scooting onto the sidewalk that connects the area with the refreshment stand. If the winter night transforms the powdery snow into something more packed, slick and fast, they have other hay bales to spread on the course in order to slow the ride. Packed, slick, and fast was what made for a memorable run down reservoir road—if you made the last turn.

Anyway, my wife, Renee, and I took my stepson, Wes, to the local inner tube sleds when he was little. He brought a few friends with him. As the night wore on towards closing time, Renee decided to take a whirl down the slope. When she started down the hill backward, I could tell she was in trouble. Then, while trying to face downhill, she found herself spinning like a top as she gained momentum. She was yelling something, but I could not make out the words. Having witnessed Tim's mystical encounter when I was 10 years old, I leaped into action and got all the kids out of the way at the bottom of the hill. Thank goodness for that, because I could see that my wife was getting some airtime on the bumps. Her hair looked like she was in the International Space Station, floating in zero gravity. Her frantic scream grew louder as she approached, I tried to see her face as she passed me, but she was spinning like a figure skater while whizzing past. Her terrified scream dopplered away, getting fainter as she plowed through the wall of hay bales like the Kool-Aid Man busting through a brick wall. To be fair, she was the only adult who had been on the course, and there was no way to know how fast an adult would go.

The staff burst into action, covering the slope in hay bales. Renee staggered out of the inner tube and picked the hay from her hair. The employees checked on her and returned her inner tube to their storage area. My wife walked up to me. "Did you see that?" she asked.

"I did. Everyone did."

"How fast was I going?"

"Probably not as fast as you think," I said, "That hill isn't very steep."

"I think I was flying!"

"Nah. You're probably just dizzy. I think you had more RPMs than MPHs."

"Really?"

"Yeah," I said, "You want to go again?"

"Heck no!" she said.

"I'll get you a hot chocolate," I patted her on the back. She would never have made it sledding with us. Anyway, these sledding trips of childhood were all big fun. Often we would take soup to cook. When I say soup, I mean we all brought a can of soup, and we mixed them all together. So, vegetable beef + tomato + chicken noodle + whatever = sled ride soup. Who knows what went into it? We would build a fire and warm it up at the bottom of the hill. It was a nice break before trudging to the top once again. At the end of my sled riding years, these trips were used primarily to find rabbits for the second small game season, which began the day after Christmas. That was also the opener for varying hare season, and back then you were allowed to shoot 2 per day. This was before coyotes had invaded the state, and you could go back into the hemlocks and find strong hare populations and have little worry of a dog being attacked. That was always my favorite part of Christmas break. Candlelight service at midnight, sleep in Christmas morning, then go look for hare tracks in the afternoon.

I didn't realize until I was older that not everyone had cottontail and hare within a short walk from their house. Keep in mind, that as a kid 6 miles was a short walk. I thought all of Pennsylvania had hare, I didn't realize it was just the northern latitudes, and only within certain pockets of higher elevation there. In the same places, we would encounter Appalachian cottontail; they run huge circles and they might make you think your hounds found a hare.

GPS has certainly made hare hunting easier. The days are mostly over when your dogs would run out of hearing and not be heard from for an hour. That can still happen, but you have GPS connection and can at least know where they are when you can't hear them.

I have hunted hare in other places—Maine, Vermont, New York, and New Hampshire. I have certainly hunted locations in each of those states that have a lot more hare than we do here in the Keystone state. Still, Christmas always reminds me of school break as a kid and the thrill of seeing a ghost-like hare sneaking through the conifers. I grew up with people who had never seen one—even though the elusive creatures were just over the hill. Somehow, they are a reminder of wild places, just beyond the familiar. I think of Christmas that way too. A wild and transforming message, that can be drowned by the shopping and cookies. The advertising lights of Madison Avenue try to overpower the light of Christ. I like the Christmas story in John. Luke has the trek to Bethlehem, Matthew has the wise men. What does John have? Some say there is no account of Jesus' birth, but there is. He has that verse 1:14, that says the Word became flesh and dwelt among us. That's the whole bit of it. The word "dwelt" comes from the Greek *skene*, and means to tent or to camp. John's Christmas story is about God going camping. Christ on earth is like when we go into the woods for a prolonged trip.

Every year I like to look at my old wooden snowshoes, a nearly 100-year old hatchet, a waterproof container for kitchen matches, and an old lensatic compass. Each was a Christmas gift from my father in my teenage years when I began taking to the Allegheny National Forest chasing the white ghosts of winter. "You never know when you will go from hunting to camping when you are out there." He would say to me.

"I've been there many times," I said.

"I know," Dad reassured me, "But you never know when a snowstorm will make everything look different.

And moving to shoot hare or catch dogs can take you to the unfamiliar places. Don't panic. Build a fire. I always remember that conversation when I read John 1:14. The Word became flesh and went camping among us.

Boots &
Belsnickel

Advent is the four Sundays before Christmas, and is a time of preparation, as we celebrate the gift of the Christ child. One of the things I have to do every year is to get five families to light the advent candle/wreath. One family for each of the four Sundays leading up to Christmas, and then another for Christmas Eve itself. It is nice to have one kid to light the candles, and another to do the reading. Dad can help steady the kid lighting the candles and Mom can assist in reading the scripture. Sometimes, I like to mix it up and have a single Mom and her kid light the advent candle. This gets raised eyebrows from some, but isn't Christmas a story about a single mother, and an unexpected pregnancy?

At any rate, when I was a kid, advent began on December 6th. Let me explain. Here in Pennsylvania, the Germanic immigrants brought this tradition of Belsnickel. Belsnickel, I am told, means something like "Nicholas in furs" or something like that. In the tradition, Belsnickel was a scruffy compatriot of Santa, and he arrived on the night of December 6th. You left your boot on the porch, and Belsnickel would bring you candy and a small toy if you were good, or kindling or coal if you were bad. Trust me, there is no shortage of kindling or coal in Pennsylvania. I am told that the older traditions might even include a visit from Belsnickel himself, who would carry a switch and possibly give you a beating. This should be no surprise, since the Germans give us the story of Hansel and Gretel, with the child eating witch; and the tale Little Red Riding Hood, a girl who encounters a wolf that has eaten her grandma. I gather that my ancestors felt that all holidays were a time to scare children. It was a cultural bias that focused on making kids productive rather than full of self-esteem. Naturally, there was no such thing as a "time out" being used as a disciplinary technique when I was a kid. Nor did my parents get me to do the right thing with positive reinforcement, AKA, give me a toy for doing the right thing. Toys, quite honestly, were mostly confined to Christmas, Easter, and birthdays. The morning of December 7th always told the tale. I would go get my frigid boot from the porch. I might get a Matchbox car or a Star Wars figure. I might get kindling,

I'm not going to lie to you, kindling was a major disappointment. It caused genuine angst to well up within you. You began questioning all of your life decisions. You began to wonder if any presents would be under the tree on Christmas. After all, Belsnickel and Santa were in cahoots together. I wouldn't say I got kindling very often, but it happened a couple times. It scared me straight until Christmas. I went out of my way to find good deeds that I could do for people in order to get back on Santa's good side.

"I got firewood in my boot," I said to my third-grade teacher, Mrs. Strauss.

"I can believe," she said and walked away. This is back when kids could flunk not just an exam, but an entire school year. Nowadays, it is almost impossible to flunk, but back then it was pretty routine. "Keep it up and you will have me for the third year in a row!" I once heard a teacher say to a kid. Teachers had paddles too, and they had them on display. If a kid got swatted with the lumber, the teacher would take the kid into the hallway for the paddling, but leave the door open so that the rest of the class could hear the impact and maybe the loud crying, depending on the kid.

I got home from school and saw Dad, who had gone to work before I woke up.

"Get a toy car?" he asked.

"Sticks," I said.

"Wow. I wonder why," he seemed shocked.

"I can't figure it out," I said, "I tried to be really good ever since Thanksgiving, to try and get ready."

"Ah," he said, "That's probably it."

"What do you mean?"

"Well, you should never be good just to get a toy. You should do the right thing because that is what you should always do. No matter what."

"Always?"

"Well, once in a great while a rule can be wrong, you know, and you have to do what is right."

"Like when?" I asked.

"Remember when I made you sit on the bench last summer so another kid could play the whole game?"

"Yeah."

"Well, you were a pretty good player, but that other kid never got to play a whole game. He always had to substitute. The way to win says that you always give more innings to your better players, but once in a while you have to help a kid out. He can't get better on the bench."

I mean, third grade seems a little young to be getting your head wrapped around concepts like the legitimacy of altruism or a deontological versus virtue-based ethical model, but there I was, in third grade, with a man who grew up with Germanic fairy tales spelling out the complexity of moral standards to me as I was thinking about a boot full of twigs.

"So what are you saying?"

"Be good," he said, "And never try to fake it. And don't do it for a toy or a reward. Just do the right thing."

I felt better right away about my twigs. "Hey," I said, "We can start the fireplace in the morning with those sticks. That isn't a bad thing."

"Good point," he rubbed my hair and walked away. Rubbing my hair was the equivalent of saying "That a boy."

It wasn't too many years after that when I was too old for Belsnickel, Santa, and those things. I got involved in beagles and hunting, and my life has gone to the dogs ever since. I still remember the year I went to college, the autumn of 1990. He bought a snow blower to clean the sidewalks, and a high-efficiency gas furnace to heat the house. Both were because his "good labor" moved to college. Kindling, before the gas furnace, was a big part

of my life, and not just in the form of punishment from
Belsnickel. We heated the house with wood for all those
years, and we got sawmill lumber to split and ignite
with newspapers every morning to get a bed of coals to
burn larger wood. The furnace wasn't connected to a
thermostat, so there were often times when our windows
were wide open, trying to get the house cool enough to
be comfortable. It happened a lot in the early fall and the
late spring. That being said, there were times when the
mercury fell below zero, the company would arrive in the
evening, the temperature in single digits, and the preferred
seats were beside the cracked windows.

Kindling chopping was a big deal. It happened every
day. We had axes, hatchets, mauls, and all sorts of things
to split everything from a big log to a tiny plank. We took
a small ax in the woods hare hunting. Dad wasn't a fan of
leaving dogs in the woods, and this was the days before
GPS collars. A hare could run out of hearing and be gone
for an hour or more before coming back. Sometimes it
never came back, and you had to go find the dogs by
walking in the same direction they were last heard, and
hoping that you heard them again. I won't say it happened
all the time, but there were a few different instances
when we caught the dogs at dark and built a fire. We sat,
sleepless until we could get enough light to head out of the
Allegheny National Forest to the truck.

In December of 1990, I came home from my first
semester of college. I was excited to be home for the hare
season, which began the day after Christmas. Naturally, I
wanted to run the dogs a bit to get some hound music in
my ears, as I had been away for months. My two dogs were
5 years old, the first dogs I ever owned. I couldn't find my
felt-lined pack boots. Well, I could find one.

"Where did I lose that other boot?" I said to no one.

"What?" Dad asked.

"I lost a winter boot. I want to take Duke and Princess
out."

"Where did you find the one in your hand?"

"Closet," I plunged back into the cluttered cubbyhole of
a room. I scrounged for a bit.

"You know," he said, "I saw a boot on the porch. I think it has been there since the first week of the month."

"The first week of the month?" I said, "you saw a boot?"

"I saw it the morning of December seventh," he said.

"Yeah," I looked him in the eye and remembered every time Belsnickel brought me kindling and every conversation that followed. I went out to the porch and found the boot, and reached inside. I felt wood. It was the handle of his old hatchet, that he got as a kid in the 1930s, and that had always been a favorite tool of mine. I used it in the house many mornings for getting fires started, but we often took it afield in the winter if we entered the big timber and might need a fire. All those trips afield, we only used it three times.

"You can have it now," he said to me.

"Really?" I asked.

"Yeah," he said, "The big woods is your place."

I didn't know he'd be dead from cancer the following August, but I think he did. So often, we let the holidays be a sad occasion because of the loss of loved ones. I try to focus on the good memories. I try to rejoice in tradition and learning. That gift from Belsnickel was the best present I ever got for any holiday. Hug the ones you love and Merry Christmas.

CHRISTMAS LETTER

There is the annual habit of sending Christmas cards to friends. Some people also include a letter that summarizes the events of the previous year, and that letter always depicts the year as having been just grand, packed full of success. I think that such letters should be brutally honest. So, here is a letter that I am going to try and sneak into my wife's cards this year. Renee may not approve . . .

Greetings everyone!

The year has flown right past us. January was a fun time since Renee and I went to Nantucket this year. No doubt, she would have preferred to go during summer, when the cold winds were not howling across the beaches. Most of the people had left the island by January, and I was able to hunt with friends. Those silly rabbits run under mansions if they get chased too long. Ha! All the same, it was great hunting since there are no land predators on the island and big open tracts of land between the mansions. I did get into some trouble because we spent a week on Nantucket and Cape Cod and never went to a restaurant. Shot lots of rabbits though!

February was the end of hunting season, and our season was extended to the end of February. I made sure to shoot a rabbit on February 29th, since it was a leap year, and I have never been able to hunt on Leap Day before. I still remember coming home after that hunt. My wife looked at the bunnies and said, "Aren't you tired of eating rabbit? You have been hunting since October." Who gets tired of rabbit hunting?

That Nantucket hunt went well in January. It went so well that Jason decided to breed his female to my Duke dog. We had tried before, but she was past her fertile time by the time we got the dogs together. After the January hunt, Jason was really eager to breed to Duke. The female, Cuddles, apparently has some sort of hormonal issue where she is no longer fertile by the time she "puts out the signals." I got her in February, and in March she was bred after a few trips to the vet to determine her peak fertility. She was almost not fertile when we were able to get her bred. Her pheromone signals came well after her peak fertility. I was not confident that she would have pups.

April ushered in a very successful trout season, though the drawback was that the beagles were not exercised very much. They were in good shape from the long hunting season, so they did not get out of condition, but they become restless from the days of inactivity. Sometimes, this resulted in sudden bursts of energy as they ricocheted around the house to expend the coiled energy in their bodies. Native brook trout are a favorite meal for Renee, so I decided to keep fishing—trout can get me on her good side. One evening they knocked a ceramic knickknack off a coffee table, and it broke. I did not have enough trout to make amends.

Remember that dog that got bred to Duke? She stayed with us until she whelped the puppies in May. It seemed easier than driving her back to Cape Cod. Boy, for almost not getting pregnant, she sure did have a big litter—6 females and 2 males. Oh, I forgot to mention that she required a C-section. That cost well over $1,000.00. Needless to say, it was a shock to my wife. My stepson was born by C-section, and I asked Renee how much her C-section cost. Although the beagle version was much cheaper, that was little consolation to my wife. Oh, the pups were born via surgery in the wee hours of Mother's Day morning after being rushed to the veterinarian the evening before, so in all the chaos I forgot to do anything for Renee. Her son, Wesley, forgot Mother's Day too.

June was a hectic month, and it culminated with a trip to Duluth, for the annual meeting of the Outdoor Writers Association of America. We left the puppies and adult dogs in the care of friends and family for the week, as we combined the work conference with a vacation. The pups were in my office with their mother. The other dogs were not nearly as cute, so our dog sitters did not spend as much time with them. While sitting in my office with puppies, one of the adult beagles knocked over a garbage can and ate some chicken bones, requiring a trip to the veterinarian to make sure he was okay. No one told us at the time, because they did not want us to worry while we were away. Since I had another vet bill, the dog sitters charged no money for staying in our house and eating chicken. Ha, it was cheaper than the C-section!

Renee had shoulder surgery in July. Her rotator cuff was bad, and they ended up scraping away part of her collarbone. She took a long time to get the anesthesia out of her system. And the surgeon as wearing cheap barn boots. Apparently, operating room floors can get very wet, which I did not know. I pointed out that he could get better rubber boots, and recommended a few brands, as I am often in the woods in wet conditions. He told me that Renee should not lift anything heavy, and walked away.

August was mostly hot, mostly unbearable, and mostly miserable. The dogs and I lived in the basement to stay cool. I kept both male puppies, and by August they were ready to chew things. How was I supposed to know that Renee kept her favorite winter shoes in the basement?

September was a good month to get the dogs in shape for hunting season, and I would often go to the beagle club to get some long chases in the morning. We did manage to get into one skunk encounter, and the dog was banished to the garage until the odor was remedied. We have one of those garages that has stuff stored in it, so you cannot park in it. The skunky dog managed to destroy an entire box and scatter the contents. It turns out that a brand-new rawhide was in the box, still in the wrapper. I thought this demonstrated a very powerful nose, but Renee saw no upside to the situation.

October brought back rabbit season and it started out with great success. One day, the hunting was so good that I had plenty of chases until dark. I was late for supper, which is not unusual, but I forgot that we were eating with my wife's boss. Ha. Wow. Well, it worked out in the end. I think.

November brought a fabulous Thanksgiving, with Renee and her Mom both cooking the same turkey for the big holiday. Naturally, they did not agree on anything. Basting the bird was a big debate, as was the temperature of the oven, the seasoning in the stuffing, the stuff that gets added to mashed potatoes, and the number of pies to make. My mother-in-law told me that she was tired of fighting with her daughter. "Keep it up," I said, "You are giving me a break."

Well, here we are in December. I am hoping to plan a road trip for rabbits next month. Maybe Kansas. Maybe Nantucket again. I am still finishing up the plans now. But I do want to wish you all a Merry Christmas, and please realize that even if want to put forth a good image of a perfect life, the reality is that Christ is with us, especially in the messiness of real life, the one we don't often advertise or tell everyone about. Blessings to you and yours in this Christmas season. And to all a good night.

CLOUD OF WITNESSES

Let's be honest, pumpkin is tasteless. It is a lot like zucchini or yellow squash that way. When we say that we like squash, what we are really saying is that we like butter. Or maybe squash that is dredged in egg and flour and then cooked in butter. When we say that we like pumpkin, we are saying that we like the stuff that goes into pumpkin pie, which is to say that we like cinnamon, nutmeg, cloves, and allspice. What is allspice? Well, it is the fruit from a tropical evergreen. Allspice adds a flavor that is a combination of nutmeg, cloves, and cinnamon, which are the other ingredients in pumpkin spice. So, you are adding more of the tastes already in the spice. I guess it is like those odd people that add salt to ham. Yeah, I saw a guy do that at a beagle club breakfast one time. This is the time of year when the world has gone pumpkin spice crazy. I walked into a coffee shop recently. I can drink any coffee, to be honest. My Mom bought whatever kind was on sale, and some of that stuff had a PH of 2. When I am doing work on my computer, I will pretend to be young and tech-savvy and utilize the wireless internet at a fancy coffee shop.

When I say a "fancy" coffee shop, I mean McDonald's on Mondays. It is free coffee, all day long. I also like their coffee. I have been to Starbuck's, and I think that they are trying to give you the taste of burnt wood. The best bear meat I ever ate was smoked. It was good, primarily, because it did not taste like bear. It tasted like the odor you get when camping and the smoke from the fire followed you around all night and then you utilize your sweatshirt as a pillow. I drink the smoky coffee too, but I like light roast better. McDonald's is nice insofar as it is easy to order coffee too. Let me explain.

There is another place I sometimes go to write and do work on my computer that is more in tune with the pop culture of today. I was there recently. "Can I interest you in a pumpkin spice latte with your choice of dairy or dairy substitute?" the gal asked me.

"Nah," I pulled cash from my wallet, "I will just get a large coffee."

"Would you like the pumpkin spice coffee?" she asked.

"Didn't you just ask me that?"

"No Sir," she looked at me as if I could not recite the alphabet, "I offered you a latte. A latte is an espresso drink with milk or a milk substitute."

"Isn't espresso just strong coffee?"

"It is not. It is made by forcing steam into concentrated coffee grounds to make a strong espresso. It is not produced by drip as coffee is." She looked at me as if she was doing groundbreaking research in the field of teaching hamsters to do remarkable things well above their intellectual capabilities.

"I see," I said, "You aren't old enough to have tried my father's coffee after it sat in the pot all day and half the water evaporated. It was very strong before it concentrated."

By now the customers behind me were getting irritated at the delay. "Just give me a cup of coffee. Throw in one of those espresso shots into it."

"So," she said, "A coffee with an espresso in it?"

"Yeah," I sighed.

"Can I interest you in a pumpkin spice scone as well?" she asked, and I nearly cried.

I wish I could say that the madness ended there. My wife is into the pumpkin stuff too. You can buy canned pumpkin and the spices all year, but apparently, it has to be consumed only during the fall. In fact, the pumpkin has been jettisoned, it is just the darn spices. It is featured in granola that is currently on top of our refrigerator where the oatmeal and cereal typically live, in a candle that lives on the mantle of the fireplace, mixed into yogurt in the fridge, and featured in cookies and other snacks in the cupboards. Heck, we have pumpkin spice salsa, which I have no intention of trying.

Autumn is about much more, and one of the days I like best is November 1, All Saints Day. In my tradition, All Saints Day celebrates all the believers who have gone to glory. It means interprets saint to mean a believer, not a morally perfect person. Other western traditions use November 2, All Souls day for this purpose. In Eastern Orthodox churches, the day is not in November at all but is the Sunday after Pentecost. This, of course, makes for extra celebrations in my state Pennsylvania (and other places too!) where we have families that follow the eastern and western calendars. This means two Easters, two Christmases, and two All Saints Days. In other words, lots of extra days to eat lots of food. This happens especially if you have relatives from both western and Orthodox churches.

Anyway, I like the idea of remembering those who have gone before, especially during autumn, when I feel connected to hunters and hound hunters who have gone before. November was always the time of year that I most associate with time afield with my dad. It has been 26 years since I have been able to share time with him, and certain things about November days afield will always remind me of him.

The smell of a wood fire, rolling from a house chimney, will make me pause and wonder if I remembered to take firewood to the basement. Apple trees will remind me of having to pick apples for my Gram, but also about having to get apple wood, for smoking meat and cheese. Apple trees, of course, are a great place to find game, including rabbits, especially if those trees are located along hedgerows of farm fields. There are computerized machines that smoke food now, but Dad would use a handmade smoker that burned wood chips. There was some specific calculus that was written down only in his mind that determined how long the wood chips should be soaked in water before being used to generate the flavor-infusing smoke. Somehow, he would calculate the variables of burn rate (wetter chips smoldered, dry ones went up in instant smoke) and outside temperature to keep a good internal temperature that cooked the meat thoroughly and yet did not "overdo" it. I can still see him now, standing in the yard, his head obscured by the warm breath from his lungs as it cooled in the winter air and encompassed him in a cloud, feeding wood chips into the burn pot of the smoker and reading the temperature gauge that he had installed into the contraption that produced all those sausages, smoked cheeses, and hams.

There was no set time for collecting wood, but throughout the year I would gather apple, cherry, and hickory wood. The pace picked up in November since there was always food prepared for Christmas the following month. My game vest would often have some apples, a dead rabbit, and some chunks of apple wood. Some days, I might just have a green limb from a cherry tree. Of course, the whole idea of All Saints and/or All Souls Day is central to Nov 1.

Tradition holds that Martin Luther nailed his famous 95 theses to the castle church at Wittenberg on October 31, 1517. It was the day before All Saints Day, 500 years ago. It sparked the Protestant Reformation. I have a puppy, that I have named Blitz, which means lightning in German. I chose the name because it is the 500th year since Luther posted his controversial statements. I chose Blitz, however, because it was during a lightning storm that Luther decided to dedicate himself to God and become a monk. Well, actually, he became a friar, which means he was active amongst people and not cloistered in a monastery. At that time the western church was united still. In other words, he was still Catholic, and not yet a Protestant, as he would be the first. The big fight that Luther started with his 95 theses was about heaven, and the ways that we can get to heaven, and if contributing money to the church could help get your relatives to heaven. Luther felt that we could not make a donation to the church to help the process, though it was a popular belief of his time.

So, this puppy, Blitz, as well as his littermate, Fang, were born in this 500th year since the debate began. If I trace their pedigrees back I can find a couple dogs from the Pearson Creek bloodline, most notably Banjo. It is back there pretty far, in the 11th generation. The same dog was in the pedigree of my original beagles, in 1985. Banjo was in the 5th generation for them. In other words, the dogs I run today are related to the first beagles I ever owned, 32 years ago. I didn't know this until I was looking over old paperwork. The fact that the dogs are distantly related is not really remarkable. After all, you could take a traditional brace hound and a small pack option or even a large pack hound and if you go back far enough you could easily find a common ancestor. Completely dissimilar dogs could have a common ancestor just a few generations ago.

Of course, All Saints Day isn't just about our relatives, it is about all the faithful who have gone before us. I think of Roger Alderman, a friend of mine who was a big fan of Yellow Creek beagles. He has been gone for a number of years now, and he and I always had the best time running dogs together. He and I once hunted a golf course in the winter when a guy asked us what we were doing. "Hunting rabbits," Roger said in a matter-of-fact voice that emphasized his disbelief that our inquisitor could not easily discern what we were doing.

"I know, the guy said as he walked through a snow drift, "But who said you could?"

"The groundskeeper."

"I am the groundskeeper, when did you ask me?"

"I asked a guy nearly 30 years ago and have been coming ever since," Roger shrugged his shoulders.

"Have a nice day," the flabbergasted gentlemen let us hunt.

Roger quit hunting in his older age and concentrated on field trialing. He had a really nice bitch that could flat out pound a rabbit. She became ill and had to be spayed. This prevented her from running in field trials, and he asked me to find a kid looking for a rabbit dog. I did. Roger gave the dog away for free. The only problem was that she had never run outside a fence. The kid and his dad had some great rabbit chases, but a few deer runs too. I got a phone call one day.

"Hello?"

"Is this Robert Ford?"

"Yeah."

"I have a beagle here that belongs to you?"

I quickly counted all the dogs in my house. It was after dark, and I was worried that there had been a jailbreak through the yard's fence and someone found my dog. The dogs were all with me.

"I think you are mistaken," I said

"Your number and name are on the collar."

I counted again. "That's weird, I said."

"She's really cute."

I suddenly figured out that the new owners must have left my collar on her. I had put one of my collars on her to get her on a leash and into my truck for transport. Where was she found? Well, she had been missing for a couple days after chasing a big deer. The caller had a garage with a fly-tying room above it. She was snuggled up on a deer hide that was used for making fly fishing flies and nymphs!

I remember Hoyt Stump, a good friend of my dad. He was older than my father and was retired throughout my childhood. Before I was old enough to drive, he would take me to the beagle club to run my dogs while he would condition his. It wasn't a year-round ride, but he would start running dogs in blackberry season. He would then pick fruit in the beagle club while his dogs—Bootsie and Pete—chased a rabbit or two. This was all in preparation for the fall hunting season. He would take me hunting in the rabbit season as well, on days my dad had to work. Hoyt has been gone for most of my adult life.

Naturally, I think of Andy Purnell. He has been gone for only a couple years. He and I did a lot of hunting, and his other friends will call and ask me to go hunting to this day.

"I have a good spot, one that Andy only told me," is something I often hear.

"Okay," I say, "Where should I meet you?"

The answer is always the same. I have had 4 or 5 guys take me to a spot that was a secret between them and Andy. I never tell them that Andy shared that spot with everyone. I always pretend that I have been introduced to a new secret. Andy and I were really good friends, and I hunted quite a few spots with him, but none of them were secrets. The secret was having good dogs.

Returning to the notion of saints. There is this idea of the communion of saints, as expressed in the Apostles' Creed. It is this idea that believers (past and present) are united across time and space. Many years ago, I wrote a paper in seminary, suggesting that we are all together whenever we take holy communion or Eucharist. The idea was that when we share bread and wine at worship, we enter a time zone. Our country has eastern, central, mountain, and Pacific time. Alaska is another hour behind Pacific, and Hawaii is two more hours behind Alaska. Travelling can move us into another time zone. Time zones, in some ways, are an arbitrary construct. I suggested that communion is like a time zone. When we go there, everyone who has ever taken communion are there. Oh, and I added all those who ever will take communion are there—people not yet born. It is what the book of Hebrews calls the "great cloud of witnesses."

A cloud of the faithful. Low lying clouds (fog) can give me this effect. All it takes is a cool morning with dense fog. A large section of thickets and briars holding rabbits next to some timber. The forest floor covered in multicolored leaf litter, the last rush of life from the trees, before the reds and oranges and yellows fall to the earth. Then comes the echoes of hound music as a pack of beagles send the age-old song of pursuit into the air. It is a song of life and death, make no mistake about it. Ask the rabbit, he knows. The hills cause a cacophony of reverberation, making 4 dogs sound like dozens. I can look at a log or rock at the edge of the tree line, as I wait in ambush at the edge of the brush. It is a border of two different places—overgrown field and forest. It is liminal, a place of transition. I await the rabbit at this spot that is not forest and not field, knowing the big running bunny will return through this permeable line. The rabbit had hopped into the big timber and hoped that the dry conditions would mask his scent, that the jumbled mix of leaves, all colors and species, would cause the pack to falter.

Four dogs sound like so many more. I can hear the voices of dogs that have long since died. Shadow, Lady, Bandit, Prince, Rocky, Duchess . . . I am sure it is just the echoes, but still. The brush and trees are familiar. I am in a specific place, but in the fog, the cloud of witnesses, it could be anywhere. It resembles places I hunted with Roger, Hoyt, Andy, and my dad. The fog is literally a low cloud of witnesses, and I can't help but wonder if the future voices are in that pack too? Puppies not yet born? It is a spot that is all places and as close as my deceased hunting companions feel, maybe the future hunters are here too. Perhaps in that fog, a great and famous breeder of beagles is waiting for this same rabbit, not a breeder of days gone by, but one whose parents have not yet met each other!

And that, my friends, is how I see a sacramental element to what you and I do. I think of Friar Luther, and how being an Augustinian meant that he went into the world to impact the lives of others. I am not opposed to cloistered work, isolated from the world, but the future is built on reaching out. All faiths can tend towards isolation rather than expansion. According to the U.S. Fish and Wildlife Service, only 5% of Americans over the age of 16 hunted in 2016. In total, 11.7 million people hunted, even if just a couple days. which is nearly 2 million fewer hunters than took the field in 2011. When I am in that fog, I have to admit that the future breeder of great beagles is not here, and I have a role to play in making sure that he or she gets here. So do you. That sacramental foggy morning renews my soul and sends me out into the world. Five percent is 1 in 20. Maybe, just maybe, I should share some of my actual secret hunting spots. Not with you, the reader of this niche magazine devoted to hunting beagles, but with a newbie. A youngster and his father. In that liminal fog where past, present, and future meet, a kid who may hold my cherished A.H. Fox shotgun hears the same rabbit I do, bounding over the dead leaves, looking backward at the pack of beagles that are relentless. He stands in the same transitional edge of the woods, where the thicket begins. Someday, in the fog of the future, I want someone to see you and me and remember our role in saving a sport that was in decline in 2017.

VOCATIONAL HOOKY

For as long as I can remember, November has gripped my soul. You know that feeling that kids get on the last day of school? Combine that with the feelings of leaving work on Friday, add a dash of birthday celebration, and you have my feelings about November, the perfect month. There was never any doubt about my love for November, and I have been finding ways to maximize the month since I was a kid. When I say maximize, I mean shirk responsibility.

My father changed work shifts every week, rotating from 11-7 to 3-11 to 7-3. At the end of each week there were two days off work before starting the next rotation, and periodically there was this thing called the "long weekend" which was really just starting work at eleven o'clock at night, giving the illusion of an extra day free from work.

When he worked the night shift, he would often hunt when he got home. He would get home at 7:15 in the morning and start loading the dogs into the truck, just as I was going to school. He could see that it was killing me to watch him prepare to hit the briars as I was beginning my walk to school. One frosty morning, I was almost out the door when he said, "Your marks good?" he looked me in the eyes with his glare that could read the soul and detect the faintest whiff of a lie or exaggeration. Dad called grades by the term "marks."

"Yeah," I confessed, "I do have a B in math, but it is a 92 right now and close to an A." The lowest A in my school was a 93. The lowest D was 70. It was back in the 1900s when teachers flunked kids. I was good at school, but then again it was a small town. It was kind of like being the second-place dog in a class of seven entries.

"You have a test today?"

"Maybe," I said.

"What does that mean?" he looked me in the eyes again.

"Sometimes the history teacher gives a pop quiz. I think it is just to avoid teaching the entire 45 minutes. It's pretty easy. He usually does that on Fridays, but it could happen today too. It could be any day."

"You want to go hunting?" he looked at me with the same piercing stare.

"Let me change clothes!" School clothes were treated like liturgical vestments. You had to keep them perfectly clean, and as soon as school was over, you removed them so they were not tainted by mundane things like play, chores, or a beagle's dirty feet. By the time I was back downstairs, Dad had loaded the dogs and we were gone. This parental sanctioned hooky wasn't common, but it tended to fall in November. Sometimes, I would overplay my hand.

"Good morning," I would say to Dad as he came in the door from work, "I have no tests today, in case you were wondering."

"I was not wondering. You already missed one day this week."

Hooky with responsibility was what we are talking about here. Sure, I skipped a few times without permission, but that was after I turned 16 and could legally hunt alone. I did it when he was working 7-3 and I began by starting to walk to school. I then circled back to the kennel where I had stowed hunting clothes, boots, and a gun the night before. Our kennel was above ground runs that led to sleeping boxes in a building. I would hang out in the building until I saw my mother's car leave to do errands, then make a feverish run behind the house and into the briars with beagles on leashes. Even those bonus days were carefully planned for days when I would not be missed at school. For $5 my sister would write my excuse to give the school nurse the next day. When I was daring, I would go to school for attendance, then sneak out the door when the bell rang for the first period, running the whole way home to get dogs.

Hooky during college was different. My father was a physically strong man but severe back pain had overtaken him during my first year of college. He was 64 years old and had enough seniority in the factory to get an easy job, in terms of labor. It was a paper mill, and he worked in the "filter plant" which was where they would draw water from the river and treat it for the purpose of making the water quality meet the standards necessary for making paper. He would test the PH of the water as well as the turbidity, and then make adjustments. There were barrels of chemicals that could be added to the water as well as bags of clay and lime. The only lifting was carrying these bags of clay and lime. I guess they weighed 50-100 pounds. It was the night shift that had to do all the lifting, to get the bags next to giant hoppers that fed the large pipes of water, as it headed into the bowels of the factory where the paper was made. The year before, I watched my dad climb a ladder with two bundles of shingles, one under each arm, as he installed a porch roof for a neighbor, making a little extra money. He installed the roof over two days in the summer, beginning after he got home from work at three o'clock in the afternoon. He stripped the old roof one day, and put down the new paper and shingles the next. In my freshman year of college, 15 months later, he couldn't lift a bag of lime without excruciating pain.

I went home on the weeks he worked 11-7 and carried all the bags. There was rarely a foreman in the filter plant, and never at night. I was missing 1/3 of my classes but was keeping up with the reading. During the November weeks when I was home, I would hunt during the day, haul bags at night. I'd sit in the main office of the water filtration plant with my father, and stare at the large gauges on the wall. They had spools of paper inside and perpetually graphed the rate of flow and other things that I cannot recall. An inked needle bobbed up and down, like a seismograph, leaving a permanent record of the day's water data.

I would then describe the chases of the rabbits that day. How the dogs did, and where they struggled. Some mornings he would hunt with me, but he sat on the tailgate and listened. His back hurt too much to hunt. Orthopedic doctors were trying to track down the pain but to no avail. "How are your marks?" he asked me, after one story I told him in the office.

I stared at the graphs, refusing to look him in the eyes. "Pretty good, actually." The truth was that I was carrying a C in calculus, and it would get worse. I couldn't do that work on my own, I needed the classroom time. I half-wondered if he knew I was lying but decided I better not change the topic. "I have 3 A's right now," I volunteered some truth, "And two classes that I think are good, but half the grade is determined by the final exams in a few weeks." He died the following summer after it was discovered that the back pain was because his cancer had returned after years of remission. I never told him about the bad grade in calculus.

In seminary, I used hooky to hunt farms owned by parishioners who worshipped at the small church I served. I attended seminary in Ohio, and while the flat terrain of central Ohio was hard to accept initially, the abundance of farmland and the good hunting felt as normal as my home in Pennsylvania. I could slip away to a large family farm and hunt anytime I wanted. There were actually several large farms that gave me permission to hunt. Even then, I could see that hooky was becoming work. Let me explain.

I work on sermons all week long. Some of that work is very much rooted in old-fashioned homework. Translating Greek or Hebrew, reading commentaries, and studying the Biblical text. Then there is the part where that academic work has to be crafted into a message that speaks to real life. At the present moment, I know a 15-year-old girl who has been taken from her parents' custody due to the sorts of things that result in the state taking a kid away. She is most assuredly dying from ovarian cancer. A kid with ovarian cancer. There is also a choir member who was riding home from her grandson's boot camp graduation at Paris Island when a basketball-sized piece of cement/ stone bounced off the highway (appearing suddenly), smashed through the windshield, broke several bones in her face, and then exited through the rear window. This was on Interstate 77 in North Carolina, where there is lots of construction. No authority there seems too concerned about finding the origin of this projectile. She was rendered unconscious initially, and her husband drove the car to look for a hospital. Thank God it did not hit him, as the car would have certainly wrecked with an injured driver. Four steel plates and 3 hours of plastic surgery followed. There is also the abundance of broken relationships, domestic violence, and natural disasters. In other words, it is all the same things that are present in the lives of all of our friends and our own families.

Hooky is now work. The outdoors is the place where I do my best to take the ancient Biblical text, which is also the living Word of God and find the best way to get a modern-day meaning. If I am honest, I admit that it is a lot of listening. I begin by listening to the hounds, and then I listen to the scripture, and I listen for whatever it is God wants me to say on Sunday. It is less like composing a message, and more like struggling to hear it, and then repeat it on Sunday morning. Somehow, that hound music puts me in the right frame of mind and acts as a conduit to something deeper. It magnifies the volume of God's message so that I can hear it. I can lose track of time, and be aware of a hunt, even if I forget much of what has transpired. It is very much like when you drive home from work, park the car, and realize you don't remember much of the drive.

I had no idea how important November hooky would be in my life when my dad took me hunting on a school day for the first time. We drove past school buses. Heck, we drove by a teacher and my dad honked the horn and waved at him because they were friends! I felt like I was getting away with something. I was breaking the rules and nobody cared. The thrill of hunting was taking priority over arithmetic and compound sentences. I could not wait to find the rabbits and put some in my vest.

Now, it is different. Don't get me wrong, I have a gun with me on those trips afield. I definitely shoot rabbits. Yet, lots of days I do not. Especially if I am struggling to hear the message and the chase is strong. When the echo of hound music bounces of the hills in a way that it sounds like two different packs of dogs singing a call and response to each other, I simply let the music bounce off me. It puts my brain in the proper place to listen and to be open to the divine. If you will excuse me, I have been studying the scriptures and I have consulted my prayer list. It is time to load up some dogs and go to work. My job has a couple hours of hooky in it today. Call it vocational hooky.

FLASHBACKS

I have no idea what happens to make a Thanksgiving Day meal go well. Well, I do in part, since we always serve wild game for the holiday and I am heavily involved in getting the meat. Some years, if I do not shoot a turkey in the woods, we do have farm raised turkey. Okay, most years we have grocery store turkey, but that is only because I am too busy hunting rabbits. To be fair, I shoot way more turkey now that we (Pennsylvania hunters) are allowed to shoot them in the fall while using dogs. There's nothing like the chaos that erupts when a pack of beagles work the thick cover that borders a field and an entire flock of turkey comes running straight at you. Driven grouse in England has nothing on beagle driven turkey in Pennsylvania.

Anyway, rabbit, grouse, woodcock, doves, squirrels, venison, pheasant, and sometimes a turkey will make the supper table. My wife cooks all of this game while I am afield looking for more rabbits. I originally began these Thanksgiving hunts because my mother and her mother were two people that should never share one kitchen. Dad and I would leave before daylight, and hunt until supper, which was late. I seem to recall a couple Thanksgivings when we were home early (noon) but that only happened in the event of the weather becoming inclement. Inclement weather, for us, consisted of a deluge that made you wonder if God might have told a guy to build an ark, and you weren't going to make the boat.

"I am soaked," Dad would say.

"I can't hear the dogs chasing!" I would yell into the downpour.

"Yeah, let's catch them when we see them."

My glasses were useless in the howling wind that blew buckets of water into my face. I took them off and put them in my pocket. It took that kind of weather to get us to go home early on Thanksgiving. One year it was cold, or at least cold for November.

"My hands are freezing and I forgot gloves," I said, "Do you think we should go home?"

"You want to watch your mom and Gram argue about gravy?" Dad asked.

"Nah," I unloaded my gun, leaned it against a tree, and put my hands in my pocket. "I'll be good in a few minutes."

To be fair, the pre-meal food was good. It was desserts, by and large. And dried corn. You could graze all day if you wanted, but that would ruin supper. The arguments over the meal were not all gravy related either. It also included basting (the frequency that it should happen), seasoning, potatoes, and pies. I had forgotten about the pie fights until recently. I mean, it wasn't the pie fight of silent movies where people threw pies in each other's face, but it was always a debate. When I say debate, I mean argument.

Marie Perreault, daughter of famed beagler Gerard Perreault, had shared a picture of her kids picking apples on social media and captioned said photograph with "Making Memories." As soon as I saw the apple picking, I had what might better be described as "flashbacks" to a youth having to pick apples for my grandmother. It was all fruit, really, but apples were the ones that bothered me the most because I was to pick them while rabbit hunting.

This was back in the 1900s when farms were common, and hedgerows were left between crops. So, you could always find rabbits between fields. Farmers left a hedgerow between their own crops and a larger one at the property line. It was fairly easy to hunt farms then, even for deer. Certainly, they had no problem with rabbit hunters. Most farms had an old apple orchard too. Very often it was not groomed or maintained anymore, so the apple production was less than in the past. These orchards were a good place to test a young dog. This was before training collars. So, it was always nice to be able to spot deer, take the dogs up to the scent line, and see how they behaved. The deer could always be found at the apple trees in the evening during late summer and early autumn. If a dog turned his head away and made a retreat from the scent, you knew the youngster was trained. If the hound took off into the woods with his head held high and tonguing the line, you then had some work to do, beginning with the process of catching the dog. You had to be fast enough to catch a dog and lucky enough to get in front of the deer. Training collars have changed everything.

Recently, one of my best dogs was at a trial with a pack that chased three different deer. On the first deer, he came back to me, knowing not to join in. It was, however, driving him crazy to listen to the chase and not join in. The dogs were caught. Soon, they jumped another deer. My dog refused to go until the pack ran within a few yards. He then joined in for a few minutes. When they started the third rabbit my dog never looked at me. All I saw was his stubby tail running up the hill. By the sounds of it, he was really getting some.

"My dog never started a deer today," I said later, "But it sounded like he was getting some checks by the end of it."

"He was driving the bus and showing the way," one judge said. Uggh.

Thankfully, in today's world, you just use the technology and in short order, the dog has been retrained. Back then we looked for deer in agricultural places to test the dogs. My grandmother lived through The Great Depression and was convinced that it was coming back in order to take a swipe at everyone again and leave banks, checks, and even cash useless. She made socks, sweaters, jackets, and gloves as if these things were unattainable. Naturally, the fruit was gathered for jellies and pies.

Apples were something she preserved in lots of ways, chief among them being apple butter and applesauce. Basically, if you make applesauce and then keep cooking it until the sugars caramelize and it gets thicker, you have apple butter. A big part of breakfast in the winter was toast, made from homemade bread, covered in jam, jelly, or apple butter. If you did not like the school lunch on any given day, you packed the same thing, except the bread wasn't toasted and you added peanut butter. If you got bored with bread, you could heap spoons of preserves into oatmeal for breakfast.

Anyway, as soon as the apples were ripe, I was sent to gather them from various farmers that would let me get them, or from wild apples in the woods. Fruit, to my grandma, should never be purchased with cash. The currency for fruit was the blood, sweat, and tears of grandchildren.

"Get back under those briars," she'd say, "You are small. Get those big blackberries in the shaded part of the bush."

"Get up to the top limbs of that tree and get the big apples!" would be a common order, "And don't you dare fall. You need both arms to press the cider." Cider was an essential part of apple butter. Instead of adding water, which she did to cook applesauce, you would add the extra oomph of sweet cider to make the butter. If you have never made cider, then imagine gathering a bushel of apples, pulverizing it, and getting a couple gallons of cider. So, not only did you have to pick the apples that went into the apple butter, you also had to get about 40 pounds of apples to make a batch of apple butter. Many batches were made every autumn.

"Look!" I would have a rabbit in my hand as I walked up to Gram, "The dogs and I got a rabbit!"

"That's wonderful honey," she would turn me around at her car and start pulling apples out of my game vest. You see, a kid could not legally hunt alone until maturing to the age of 16, so my grandmother would sometimes take me hunting after school at local farms. Naturally, my dad would take me if he was home, but his work schedule did not always permit an afternoon hunt. My Mom would take me too, but she was very appreciative to not go. Gram was my rabbit uber. Instead of calling for the ride on the cell phone, you arranged the ride the night before. The fee was apples.

I had to fill the game vest in return for the ride, and that was always a hassle when I was trying to shoot a rabbit. The chase would start coming back to me, and I would jump out of the tree and load my gun. Gram was loading apples into buckets at the same time. When I was 14 my father gave me a coon hunting light.

"Just hunt until dark, then pick a bushel for her," he said, "leave the light and the basket in her car until you are done hunting."

On Thanksgiving, my mother liked pumpkin pie, and my Gram liked pumpkin roll. Also, Grandma preferred fruit pies over both. Apple pies were a fixture of holiday meals. Some apples were stored in a fruit cellar, others were simply peeled, sliced, and frozen for future pies. If it rained hard on Turkey Day, and we quit hunting rabbits early, it was always a time to eat desserts on the porch. I often preferred nut roll, which is another story (black walnuts, beechnuts, and chestnuts were foraged).

"Hey, is this rain going to quit by Monday," I asked my dad as we sat on the porch.

"I hope so," he pulled his hat low against the drizzle blowing onto us during the occasional strong gusts of wind. My mother's voice came through the porch door, which was closed, "We only have one oven, Mom!" Her and Gram were having another debate about the temperature of the oven.

These memories filled my mind and I was thinking about them as the dogs were running a rabbit recently. I was hunting an old apple orchard, and the rabbits were running pretty well. The orchard was overgrown and the high cover made it hard to see the rabbits. I did manage to shoot one bunny. As I put it in my vest, I realized that I had packed the vest full of apples. I did it subconsciously, as I was remembering Thanksgiving feasts from the past. I took the apples into the house when I got home.

"What do you want me to do with these?" my wife, Renee, asked.

"There's not enough for apple butter."

"You don't think I am making apple butter, do you?"

"Nah. Maybe a pie."

About a decade ago, an older gal at church taught my wife how to make homemade pie crust. It makes all the difference, really. I thought I was having flashbacks about apples, but I guess it truly was memories. I am glad there was no social media then. A picture of me in the top of a tree would look like child abuse today.

THE FIRST DAY

I can still recall my first day of deer hunting. It was a November Monday, I was 12 years old, and I did not sleep much the night before. I know that I dozed off for a few minutes because I woke up at 4:30 in the morning, worried that I had overslept. I went downstairs, and too excited to eat breakfast, I drank some orange juice and waited for my father to come downstairs. There was no deer camp, we lived a couple miles from where we hunted.

The same thing had happened a few years earlier when I went trout fishing for the first time. I slept a little longer since you have to wait until eight o'clock in the morning to begin fishing on the first day. I am not sure what the reason is for that rule, but the same is also true for the first day of pheasant season in Pennsylvania.

I was very excited to go for those first trout and my first deer hunt. I was even more excited to go rabbit hunting for the first time. I had been training my own beagle and my father had a half-littermate. I had been watching those dogs make nonstop circles for many months. I had stood motionless and silent, just as Dad had told me, trying to get a glimpse of the bunnies as they crossed the paths of the beagle club.

"There won't be mowed paths like this when we go hunting," my dad said as I pointed at a running rabbit. My childhood was, as my stepson says, way back in the 1900s. Back then you couldn't train dogs in the wild during the summer months in The Keystone State. Beagle clubs were the only place you could really condition dogs, the idea being that hunting dogs training in the wild would kill large numbers of baby animals. Good science has proven those notions wrong, and we can now train on public lands all year.

Right away I learned how much harder it was to see rabbits. I could hear them running, but could not see them. "Sometimes you just have to know that it is going to take a little while," my father said as I peered into the tall weeds, "If it doesn't go in a hole, the dogs will keep circling it. Be patient and find a spot where you can see him if he passes. But don't stand where it is too open. It has to be enough cover that he can stay mostly hidden, but you can also see him sneaking.

In the weeks leading up to the opening day, I would see rabbits running far in front of the dogs. They would stop in front of me and lick their feet momentarily. Sometimes they would double back on their own scent trail, pausing for just a second as they turned around. Even before I had shot a rabbit, I knew that those were easy shots. Then, the night before my first hunt with beagles arrived.

When I was 5 or 6 years old I had every intention of staying awake to catch Santa Claus in the act of leaving presents. I put on a vigil from the couch right beside the Christmas Tree. I awoke at four o'clock in the morning, in my bed. The presents were under the tree. I was more excited for my first rabbit hunt than I was about any Christmas presents. I couldn't wait to have those dogs perform wonders, and for rabbits to fill my game vest.

I wanted to sleep. I figured I would get tired if I just pulled the blankets up over my head and turned out the lights. I was a known reader, and I would often have a flashlight to read hunting magazines or Pat McManus books. After four chapters, I realized I wasn't falling asleep. So, I made sure that I had all my gear ready for the morning. After all, I had only checked it four times before trying to go to sleep. I slipped downstairs and into the laundry room, which doubled as a back porch/coatroom. I reached into the vest and found the magazine for my shotgun. Yeah, you read that correctly, my shotgun had a magazine.

It was a bolt-action 20-gauge with a magazine that held two rounds. It could hold one round in the action. It was made by *Western Auto*. My father would have insisted that

I use a hinge action single shot, since he felt that a pump or autoloader or even a double barrel was (1) too expensive to buy a kid that was still growing, and (2) encouraged rapid fire. I bought the gun with my paper route Christmas tips. It was used, and cost $60. Naturally, I had been reading all the hunting magazines I could find. There wasn't a lot of attention paid to rabbits, but there were lots of articles on bird hunting. After reading all I could about shot size I decided to put a #6 shot into the magazine first, and then a #7 ½. I figured I would use a #7 ½ in the action as well. The idea was that the #6 would have more oomph and punch and would be my third and last shot as the rabbit got further away. I had target practiced with the gun, but I had never really considered how long it took to get to the third shot with a bolt action shotgun. I liked the bolt action because it had more rounds than the single shot hinge action. Dad liked it because the safety was more reliable, and practically speaking it was still a single shot. You did not even get a second shot unless the first one had really wounded the rabbit.

I took the shells out of the magazine to make sure that they were in the right order. They were, just like the dozen times I had checked before. I checked my leash next. I had a fancy leather lead, made by Blett in Sunbury, PA. That manufacturer was a big deal back in the 1980s. It was a standard four-foot long leash. The leash hung on a hook in the laundry room, ready to go get dogs for the transport from the kennel to the truck. When worn diagonally across my body in a loop with the French snap attached to the hand-held loop, the top rested on my left shoulder and the bottom touched my belt, on the right side. I now order the leashes five feet long, so that they fit me as they did when I was a kid.

I had two fluorescent orange hats, and both were at the ready. My rubber boots sat in the corner, right under the hook that held my "duck" shirt. This, of course, was a cotton duck shirt, but we just called it a duck shirt. Heavy and briar proof, they are the staple of all rabbit hunters. I had one, and so did my father. It was an outerwear garment that was mostly washed by the elements. I

checked the pockets of my duck shirt to make sure that
I had my fire starter in there. For some reason, probably
due to reading hunting stories, I always had this odd
sort of feeling that I would be stranded in the wilderness
and have to start a fire. I gained wisdom as I aged and
stopped carrying fire starter. Then, I dang near got lost in
a Vermont swamp in the Northeast Kingdom, and I now
carry fire starter again. I had to gain more wisdom to be as
wise as when I was a foolish kid.

I walked back into the house to look at the lunch I had
packed. I figured three sandwiches and 2 packs of crackers
would be enough. I guess I planned on eating lunch and
supper in the woods. My dad was giggling slightly as
I packed the meal the previous evening. I checked my
thermos to make sure the water was still hot. I filled it with
fresh hot water, to preheat it before the morning cocoa
went into it. Dad's thermos sat beside mine, it would hold
coffee. I changed the hot water in it too.

My "duck" pants were ready, neatly folded and resting
on the floor of my bedroom. My shotgun was there as well,
cleaned twice since I last shot it. Half a box of shells sat
with the cardboard lid open on my dresser. I checked my
wallet for cash, as I wanted to be able to buy a pop (maybe
it is called soda where you live) if we drove past a gas
station in the afternoon. Next to my wallet was a pocket
knife, and I opened the blade to test it for sharpness. I
was constantly touching up the edge and spent more than
a little time whittling sticks. I walked back downstairs to
look for the wool socks that my grandmother made. Sure
enough, they were in a clothes basket with some of my
other garments, waiting for me to take them upstairs. I was
so fidgety with anticipatory energy that I took the whole
basket upstairs without being asked. I was the only one
awake and went back downstairs to get a snack. I watched
the television quietly. At 5 o'clock in the morning, I decided
to get my duck pants on and wait for Dad to wake up. I
had a bowl of cereal and went back to sit on the couch.

I woke up to the unmistakable sound of an engine. I
opened my eyes and saw Dad was driving the truck and I
was in the passenger seat. "What is going on?" I asked.

"Last night I remembered a good hunting spot on a farm. It is an hour drive, so I decided to let you sleep," Dad said.

"Oh," I rubbed my eyes, wondering where my glasses were.

"I figured you were up all night," he answered my internal thoughts, "Your glasses are on the dashboard and your boots are on the floorboard. Your wool socks are inside them."

I glanced around and noticed that I was sitting on my duck shirt, and my vest and gun were in the cap-covered bed of the truck. "I don't remember going to the truck."

"Ha!" Dad snorted, "I carried you to the truck like I carried you to bed on Christmas Eve as a little kid." I was embarrassed to tell anyone that when it happened, but it just seems like a fitting start for a rabbit hunter. I like to think I do not get that excited before the first day of the season anymore, but I do. I still go over the equipment. I still look forward to getting rabbits. I have a better gun. I fuss over GPS tracking collars these days. If only someone was big enough to carry me to the truck when I stay awake too late! The first day is almost here.

DIRTY

Well, it is autumn, and time to winterize here in the north. This was a big production when I was a kid, as my father had made customized storm windows. They were made for the back porch, which was the staging area for heating the home. Firewood was stacked in our yard. The back porch held enough fuel for a couple weeks. The wood stove was in the basement, and we generally stacked enough wood to last 4 or 5 days down there. So, the wood moved closer and closer to the fire until it was burned. The storm windows were so that you could stay reasonably warm since the porch was connected to the basement. The house was built without a basement, but my father jacked the house up in the air, hand dug the dirt (clay) from under the house, poured the basement walls and floor, and then lowered the house. He installed stairs to enter from the yard, enclosed those stairs and connected them to the porch. The storm windows kept the back porch free from snow, and you could go to the basement in slippers and a long-sleeved shirt to feed the fire. To be honest, it was a cellar, not a basement. What is the difference? A cellar has no finished walls, no furniture, contains many shelves filled with canned food from the garden, and occasionally leaks when it rains hard.

October was time to put up the storm windows and can jelly. Mom and grandma froze fruit all summer. Then, in preparation for hunting season, the fruit was removed from the freezer. Usually, there would be a pie or two made and the rest were preserved as jelly. The freezer was then ready for rabbits, grouse, squirrel, and deer. It was also the time when we waged the endless war on the leaves. You can rake your leaves, but when the wind blows you find that you will acquire all the deciduous droppings from the nearest neighbor to your west. And every other leaf that once was west of your house.

As kids, we would rake them into huge piles in the front yard and then jump off the banister, which encircled the front porch, into a soft pile of oak and maple leaves. The leaves would break your fall, and you would do it again. I told my stepson, Wesley, this story when he was a kid, in the hopes he would rake the remains from the massive maple tree in our yard. Not long after he grabbed the rake, he came in the house sobbing.

"Bob, why did you tell me to do that?"

"What?" I asked.

"Jump in the leaves! It hurt?"

"You're kidding?" I said in disbelief and walked into the yard. The lawn was covered with leaves, with one tiny pile by the porch.

"Dude!" I said to Wesley, "You have to put all of the leaves in the entire yard into the pile. Of course, those few leaves weren't enough!"

"You didn't say that!"

"Well," I said, "Rake up the rest of the leaves and try it again." I decided that I shouldn't tell him that when the leaves were abundant we would get on the porch roof and jump. Raked leaves from my youth were then collected into a pile after a rain and burned. The ash was put in the compost pile. One year, Dad decided to make customized storm doors for the dog kennel. The sides were enclosed with plexiglass, and the doors had plexiglass shutters that could be closed, or held open with eye hooks. I saw the dogs lazing on the wire runs as the sun poured through the clear plexiglass, while temperatures dipped below zero on a cold, cloudless day with northern air swooping down. Of course, the wire runs led to a heated shed that my dad built. They may have been out on the wire runs to cool down! Those dogs had life pretty good.

My modern fall preparation is far less complicated. I wait until the wind stacks the leaves against the house, and then I attack them with the lawnmower.

"You mow the leaves better than the grass," My wife, Renee, said to me.

"It doesn't grind them all," I answered.

"Well," she said, "you don't mow the leaves better, just more often."

"I have bigger fall preparation," I said.

As the leaves are not getting raked, I often find myself using October as the scouting season. In the winter I look for rabbit tracks in the snow and make mental notes of potential new hunting spots. October is the time when I test these new spots, taking the dogs afield to see how strong the rabbit population is. Our hunting season begins the last Saturday in October. I now have a new problem. My truck has been so customized for dogs that it is useless for work. The bed is full of dog box, there is a tent on top of a ladder rack, and the bumper is full of storage boxes for tracking collars, dog food, water bowls, tie out stakes, and other gear. In other words, it is easily noticed. Every local guy with a beagle follows me to find my hunting spots.

So, I recently borrowed my wife's car to evade any followers. It's a Toyota, Rav 4, and has four-wheel drive. Let me tell you, the clearance is not as good as my truck, which I determined by getting high centered on a road with deep ruts. Also, there is no dog box in that SUV, so the dogs just rode in the back seat, and the upholstery became covered in dog hair.

"What happened to my car?"

"It's just dirty."

"Dirty!" she yelled, "The whole thing is covered in mud!"

"Yeah, but I got the stuff from underneath. Transmission and drive train was packed in mud."

"Why?" she shrugged her shoulders, and I had the distinct impression that I should not have told her about the undercarriage getting so muddy when I was bogged down in the ruts. I got the garden hose to wash her grocery fetching 4X4. Renee supervised. Clumps of mud fell to the driveway. A stream of brown water rolled into the street.

"Why aren't the windows getting clean?" she asked.

"They are," I said.

"No," she shook her head, "Look, they are not." She pointed at the passenger window.

"Ohhh," I said, "That."

"Yeah," she grimaced, "That."

"Well," I began.

"Well what?" she interrupted.

"That is on the inside."

"On the inside of what?"

"Inside of the window," I said. I could see that she was trying to say something, so I answered her before she stopped stuttering. "That is from the dogs rubbing noses on the windows." She opened the door to look.

"The hair is everywhere."

"Well," I said, "They always go nuts as soon as the wheels leave the pavement. But in my dog box, they contain the excitement to a degree. They ran all around that car looking out the windows for rabbits. So they got some slobber and nose smudges on the glass."

"On every window?"

"Oh yeah," I answered, "It was kinda hard to drive there for a second or two."

"Why didn't you use a plastic crate?"

"They were in the basement," I said, "It would have taken too long."

"Not as long as it will take you to clean this mess."

"I have to mow leaves, can I clean it later?"

"You can clean it now. I have to carpool with people in this car tomorrow."

It only took two hours. It would have taken less than five minutes to put some plastic crates in the backseat.

VACATION
HOT SPOTS

I have taken my wife, Renee, to some pretty popular locations. Not long after we were married I took her to the fabled Finger Lakes. "Want to go to the Finger Lakes for the Day?" I asked.

"Sure!" she said, my favorite winery is there."

"Okay," I said.

We traveled along and chatted. As we got close she said, "What lake are we going to?"

"Cayuga," I said.

"This seems like an odd way to get there."

"Yeah," I said, "I never seem to get there the same way twice."

The minute I got on a dirt road my wife said, "I hear dogs."

"Yeah, I said, "Dirt roads excite them."

"Why do you have dogs?"

"I have always had dogs. You knew that."

"I know, but why are they with us at this moment?"

"Oh," I said, "You didn't see me put them in the dog box?"

"Umm, no."

"Oh," I said, as I turned into Cayuga Lake Beagle Club.

"We are nowhere near a lake."

"Nah, but we can stop and look for your favorite wine on the way home."

"A field trial," she said.

"Oh yeah. And they have a few snowshoe hare here."

She has also been to the Berkshires. She has traveled to Cape Cod. She even made a trip with me to Nantucket. She walked the cobblestone streets of the island while

I was hunting rabbits on public land. She has been to several trials at Cape Cod Beagle Club.

"I have been to Cape Cod 4 times and never ate in a restaurant or shopped in a store," she said to me.

"Oh yeah?"

"Yeah. Can we eat something besides rabbits the next time you go hunting at Cape Cod."

"We cooked that fancy sausage that Jason Wiseman bought. Portuguese linguica it was called."

"Yeah, the next time you shoot rabbits on a beach, I want supper in a restaurant." Lately, I have been thinking of some other fancy destinations. For instance, maybe Myrtle Beach could be a good vacation. From there I could locate marsh rabbits, a species I have never hunted. Surely, she would like Myrtle Beach.

There is the Alaska Hare, a tundra species larger than the snowshoe hare I usually hunt. I am told that they hunt jackrabbits from horseback since the dogs will take them in such huge circles. I asked my wife about this.

"Can you ride a horse?" she asked.

"Kinda," I said.

"Can you kinda ride and shoot?"

"Hmm. Good question."

"You can kinda fall off it."

"Good point," I said, "Superman fell off one and was paralyzed. He knew how to ride and wasn't shooting a gun."

"What?"

"The guy that played Superman. I forget his name."

"Well, you have plenty of rabbits here."

She is right. Not long ago we went to a field trial at New England Beagle Club, one of the oldest clubs in the country, established in 1893. Before we left, she was on the phone with her mother.

"Mom, we are traveling for our anniversary." There was a pause, and I do not know what her mother said.

"Umm, we are going near the Berkshires."

Pause.

"It's really nice, I think, I have never been there."

Pause.

"In a tent."

Pause

"I said in a tent."

Long Pause.

"I love you too."

"It is nice there," I said, "They have a few hare too!"

Off we went to camp and run dogs.

Chasing bunnies and hunting has taken my wife to all sorts of places.

"What do you think of California?" I asked.

"I go there for work conferences," she said.

"Dessert cottontail," I said.

"You want to haul dogs to California?"

"I am thinking about it."

"Take horseback lessons. Go for the Jackrabbits."

"I love you."

LUNCHBOXES & SNEAKERS

It is definitely that time of year when school is on everybody's mind. This is my experience of the school year, as someone who routinely interacts with parents of children. In May, they all say, "I cannot wait until the school year is over, so I do not have to fight with these kids to wake up every day." By the beginning of August, they are then saying, "School can't start soon enough! Having these kids around the house all day is driving me crazy." Since most families have two working parents, daycare must be arranged.

I live 45 minutes from State College, home of Penn State University. There are cultural differences it the 40 miles between that more urban town and the borough of less than 500 people where I live. First of all, State College has lots of commuters that use a bicycle, and people who get around town faster that way for daily errands, since the traffic has the volume of a big city packed into a big town. These are cyclists that wear spandex to pedal 10 miles, and then utilize a gym in their office building to shower and change into work clothes. For the most part, middle-aged guys and gals on bicycles where I live have been convicted of DUI and no longer have a driver's license. Sometimes they get another DUI on a bicycle. One guy got a DUI on a lawn tractor. Not sure if he was inspired by George Jones.

Daycare is very different too. In State College, there is such a demand for these services that there are daycare centers and then there are places that function as a prep school to get your infant into college. None of them are inexpensive, and it is not at all uncommon for a couple to dedicate the entire salary of one parent (and part of the other parent's paycheck) to paying the daycare bills. This, of course, is to allow both parents to continue advancing their careers, the financial loss for daycare ends at kindergarten.

Where I live, the daycare duties fall upon grandparents. Half sleeping kids get dropped off at grandma's house in the morning, and then they are retrieved after work. Some kids get to grandma and grandpa's house after supper and sleep there so as to eliminate the hassle of loading and unloading slumbering children. I talked to one Grandfather in late August. We were running dogs in the evening together. He and I were talking pleasantly about the chase, kidding each other about who had better dogs, and having a good conversation. Then I asked him, "Are the grandkids ready for school?"

His face turned sullen. He appeared to age 10 years in 10 ten seconds. His shoulders hunched forward. His eyes starting blinking rapidly. "Oh," his voice sounded weaker and gravely, "They are not ready but I am!"

"Yeah?" I asked.

"I worked in a factory for 45 years! These ten-hour shifts of babysitting are killing me."

"The pay is good though," I joked, "Right?"

"I'd punch you if you weren't a preacher."

"Ha! Good one," I said, "Your joke was better than mine about the good pay."

"I ain't joking."

Back to school means a lot of things. In part, it means getting ready for the school year. New clothes, new backpacks, and new lunch boxes were part of the game when I was a kid. Clothes shopping, then and now, was never something I liked. My mother did laundry every Wednesday. So, I had three pairs of school pants. This was enough for five days of school. I received five new shirts so that I wore a different one each day of the week. I had five identical pairs of blue jeans, so no one knew I wore some pairs twice per week. I got five shirts because we didn't want to look poor by having just three. There was usually another shirt or two that was in good condition from summer that could be worn to school as well.

Of course, there was a brand-new pair of sneakers. The first day of school smelled like you were standing in the middle of the clothes rack at Sears, and sounded like ten simultaneous basketball games as the new sneakers squeaked on the freshly waxed hallway floors. The minute I got home from school I had to change clothes. I was sent to my room like a West Nile virus patient being quarantined.

"Don't forget to change your socks too!" my mother would yell up the stairs, "Do not get mud stains on the new ones!" I would change into an old shirt and a pair of jeans that had at least one patch sewn onto it, frequently more. When you outgrew denim, it became patches. I could then go outside to play, take beagles to the briars, or eat food. Mom was always upset if I ate an afterschool snack and spilled something on my good clothes, which is why I had to change immediately. I was always happy to change into my "play" sneakers, since they were broken in well, and felt more comfortable.

Lots of kids, especially in more suburban places, do not play outside any more. There are reports of kids in New Jersey who have not seen the sun in their entire lives and have evolved large eyes to see computer screens better in the low light conditions of their houses. Even where I live there is a decrease in playing outside. Because of this, I am not sure that there is still a division within wardrobes that could be characterized as "school" versus "play" clothing.

I was a bit of a nerd as a kid. Okay, I was a total nerd. Therefore, I enjoyed getting school supplies more than I did clothes. I liked getting mechanical pencils, rulers, and graph paper. As I went through high school I ended up taking every science class that the school district had. I especially liked getting the newest scientific calculators.

"It costs how much?" my dad would shake his head as he pulled out his wallet. Dad carried cash. He had one check in there, just in case he needed to make a major purchase at a hardware store or something. It was usually discolored from being in there for several years.

We are currently in the back to hunting time of year, and as adults, we still need to get new stuff for the fall. After all, you may have worn out your old hunting clothes.

Or outgrown them (it happens). We all need to get ready for the school year. I mean rabbit season.

Overalls

In the past couple of decades, I have become a big fan of bibs for hunting. In large part, this is because I tend to hunt for an hour every weekday morning before going to work. I pretty much have to wear khakis or dress slacks. Filson tin bibs are briar proof. I can slide them over a pair of Dockers and they keep my work pants rip free and mostly wrinkle-free. After a quick rabbit hunt, all I need to do is remove the overalls, change shirts, and put on dress shoes. I also like Mule brand bibs a lot, but only in the winter, since their waterproof products tend to get hot, especially in the early season. Stone Creek Hounds and Supplies also have a great product.

Sling

I am not a fan of slings on shotguns, especially since I shoot birds over my beagles as well. It is not easy to take a gun from being slung on your shoulder to mounted on said shoulder fast enough to hit a flushing bird. However, when you are leaving the field with a pack of beagles, it is also not easy to hold leashes and a shotgun. There are a variety of holsters that can be attached and removed with no hardware. They vary in price, and you can choose one based on your preference in materials and budget. I have a middle of the road model, made by Levy's Leather. I keep it in my vest pocket, and can quickly attach it to my double barrel shotgun to free up hands for leashes on the return to the truck.

Bells

I love GPS, but batteries fail, and signals get blocked. I use a low tone, Canadian made Bell that I buy at Lion Country Supply. Last year, while in Maine, with the topography and wind working in my favor I heard the bell at over 300 yards. Typically, I can hear it for 150-200 yards. Additionally, a bell keeps your dog safe when hunting in areas where you may encounter the dangerous small game hunter—the guy that shoots at moving brush (it is always a guy, not a woman hunter).

Permethrin

I don't go in the woods without this stuff on my outer layer of clothing. There are various manufacturers. Tick-borne diseases are getting worse. Have you heard of Powassan? It can be transmitted in just 15 minutes from the time the tick attaches to you (unlike Lyme, which takes 24 hours) and in some cases, it causes encephalitis which is often deadly. Go for the permethrin.

Boots

I no longer go afield without boots that are tall enough to tuck my pants into. More specifically, they have to be tall enough that my pants do not become untucked. This is because of ticks, and a several tick encounters with the nasty arachnids that required medical attention. I have a rubber pair for wet days and mornings, a leather pair for warm afternoons, and an insulated pair for winter. It has made a big difference and kept the ticks at bay. Mostly.

Dasuquin

This stuff is sold by veterinarians and dog supply stores. It is a joint supplement that really helps aging dogs rebound during the days that we are running them hard. You can give it to young dogs at a maintenance level, which can add a couple extra years of good performance to your hound if taken over a lifetime. I get the best prices on Amazon. There are other manufacturers of products that contain the same ingredients—glucosamine hydrochloride, methylsulfonylmethane, and sodium chondroitin sulfate. You may want to shop around for other manufacturers.

Bore Snake

Of course, I should clean my shotgun every time I use it. I do it more often now, since the invention of the Bore Snake. The snake has 160 times for surface area than a gun cleaning patch and has a brush built into the fabric.

It takes ten seconds to clean the bore. They are gauge or caliber specific.

Lunchbox

Remember that great lunchbox and thermos as a kid? I had a Star Wars one. They now make these giant travel mugs for coffee that fit in your truck's cup holder. It holds enough coffee for the day and stays hot. I use a Yeti brand, although there are others. They all seem to keep it hot until evening. If I hunt all day and return to the truck for lunch I have hot coffee waiting in the same mug I used driving to the hunting spot hours ago. Heck, I have kept soup warm inside of one. These same companies also make new generation coolers. The small ones are perfect for a lunchbox. After I have eaten lunch, I transfer the ice packs to an older cooler where I put the field dressed rabbits and birds. The game cooler isn't used for food anymore, but I still clean it thoroughly to keep it free from tularemia and other diseases or parasites.

Well, I hope you get to do a little back to hunting shopping while the kids are getting sneakers and lunchboxes. I am going to go afield now, and I want to leave early. The busses are back on the roads in the mornings. I hope your kids and grandkids have a great school year, and thanks to all the teachers.

PRESEASON

Perhaps, if you live in rural America like me, you have dwindling class sizes in your town as the school year begins. A few years ago, the district where I work had a class of 6th graders with only 11 boys. There were more than 20 girls in the grade. Those kids are about to enter junior varsity, and it causes troubles for the football coach, I am sure. On the other hand, there shouldn't be any boys having trouble getting a date for the prom in a couple years. For a couple decades, we have been facing the reality that our kids graduate and move. They either go to college and do not come back, or they go straight into the workforce and do not come back. Granted, there are exceptions, but our community is getting older and the commutes to work are getting further.

I graduated with 88 kids way back in the 1900s. There were enough kids that it was tough to make the team. I am not saying that I played every year of sports, but I played a couple years of football. The coach would look at the scoreboard. "Hey, Ford! Come here."

"Yeah, coach?" I would run over.

"How many points are we winning by?"

"Can't you see the board?"

"Yeah. Says 64 to 6."

"Okay then," I said.

"So how many touchdowns?"

"Umm. nine touchdowns and a couple two-point conversions." This was before soccer was popular. There wasn't a lot of extra points or three-point field goals. You scored 6 for the touchdown, and you either made the two-point conversion or you didn't. Now, most teams have a soccer star that kicks for the football team and all sorts of things can happen.

"Nine touchdowns?" Coach said, "Not even you can't mess that up. Strap up your helmet and go in for the last minute."

"Thanks, Coach. What position?"

"No one cares."

"Okay."

Now, playing time gets determined by how many kids are available. This is true for all sports. Some school districts, once rivals, now combine athletic departments to get enough players to field a team. My squad of beagles is like that. There are only four, so they are all starters. Duke, Hoss, Badger, and Rowdy. In other words, they all make the team. Oh, I also have two pups (Fang and Blitz), the redshirt freshmen. They were born in May, and I hope to put them in the game this winter.

Duke is 7 and has lost half a step, but is probably still my best current dog in terms of not losing a rabbit. If there is a long check that I fear may become a loss, it is often his rolling bawl that tells me the chase is still very much alive. Hoss, Duke's littermate, has also lost a half-step in terms of his speed. It has greatly helped him, actually. He was once so eager to take the front he would do some silly things. Middle-age has treated him well, in terms of his performance on a bunny. Big Badger is now four, and my real star. He is in his prime, and while Duke may get more tough checks, that is only on days when a tough check occurs. Badger can push a rabbit hard enough that it doesn't get a chance to get tricky, and he is a pretty good check dog himself. Rowdy is three years old and a late bloomer of sorts. He belonged to my friend, Andy Purnell, and was just a pup when Andy died. I got Rowdy when he was a year old and not started on rabbits. Andy's wife wasn't able to get him afield, and I acquired the dog. He is getting better, and I hope he improves.

"Rowdy," I said the other day, and he ran to me, "Dude, you should be on the practice squad. I need you to put it together before the little pups take your spot." Rowdy has been showing some signs of improvement, but it is because I have been letting him develop at a slower pace. It is tough on him to run with the more experienced dogs. Right now, he is like the kid that is a junior in high school and still playing junior varsity. But I think he may become a very good hound, albeit with slower development. Perhaps he will be a great player next year.

September is the intense part of my pre-season. The weather has shifted towards autumn enough to give me some cooler days so that I can condition dogs and see what I have. I tend to go to field trials in the spring when my dogs are pretty tough from the rigors of hunting season. I live in Pennsylvania, and my dogs are in the house, so they get a fair amount of air conditioning in the summer. As a result, they tend to overheat a little faster. July and August are down months for me. Also, many of the spots where I condition dogs could contain a rattlesnake or two. Chasing rabbits in the snake-prone summer heat to maybe get a ribbon is something that worries me. I will attend a few trials in September, and run dogs most mornings.

When I was about 10 years old I was playing summer baseball. The kid that could throw the ball the hardest, Mike Sherry, was on our team. To be honest, it was a blur. You had to make up your mind early if you wanted to swing. Also, I was a little bit afraid. But, he pitched to me at practice, and no one on the other teams threw as hard as he did. Oh, and he hit me in the arm, thigh, and helmet. Not on purpose, mind you, but we were 10. Accidents happen. So, a few bruises later I got over it and was able to hit pretty well when facing other pitchers in the league. It helped to practice with the best.

I feel that way about beagle club rabbits. They get chased every day. They are tricky. Taking my small squad to run those professional rabbits makes them look even better in the wild on bunnies that never saw a beagle. Every time my pack gets defeated by the best club rabbits I try to be optimistic and say, "But they will never lose one in the wild." Sure, I am wrong, they will lose a few rabbits during the hunting season, but they will look so much better from having practiced with the best. Like getting hit in the leg with a Mike Sherry fastball.

I tend to go on the road. I like to try new states and new species of rabbit. Going on the road presents its own problems. As I said, I live in Pennsylvania. I grew up in the western part of the state when Pitt and Penn State not only had competitive teams back then but also played against each other every year. It was a Saturday when people got really uppity and aggressive as they cheered for one team or the other. I went hunting and didn't care who won. Anyway, there is a famous story about Woody Hayes bringing the Ohio State Buckeyes into State College, PA to play Penn State. I am familiar with the airport, as it is the one I utilize on the rare times that I fly. It is in the ridge and valley region of the state. Frequently, the final approach brings you over one of my hunting spots. It can be windy on a good day.

So, in 1976 the Buckeyes were coming to play football and the weather in the hills was less than ideal. It was suggested that they land at a larger airport and bus to the game. The bus would have added several hours to the commute, so Hayes considered his options. There were two small planes, due to the small size of the airport (even now there are only two gates, I think. Maybe three). One plane had the coaches and the first string. The other had the backup players and the administrators. As the story goes, Coach Hayes ordered the second plane to land. The reasoning was that if that plane made it, he would then follow with the first string. I sometimes think this is the way people travel with dogs to attend trials and hunts, with little concern for the hounds. I hate to see a light, plastic crate in the bed of the truck that could be easily launched into the air from an automobile accident. Or dogs are packed into a dog box so tightly that they can overheat.

I try to take care of the athletes in the back of my truck. I like a box that is well insulated (from heat and cold) with good ventilation. It should be anchored in some way so that it does not escape the truck in the event of an accident. So often dogs are packed into boxes such that there can really be a problem if you are stuck in slow traffic. Tailpipe exhaust could be deadly in gridlock traffic, so I worry about adequate ventilation. I also take the trouble to find places to let dogs relieve themselves. It is not good to drive for 12 hours without letting the hounds water some local shrubbery. It can be hard to take time to walk dogs, but I think it is important on longer trips. I do not have a second string of athletes to sacrifice at the local airport like Hayes gambled with his human players, and would not do so if I did.

Lastly, it is worth noting that the dogs are not that much of a reflection on me. If they do poorly, it does not mean I am a bad person. If they do well, I am not the one who was competent—the dogs were. I find it sad when I go to a local high school game and it is clear that a parent is deriving every bit of their self-esteem from a kid on the field. I feel worse for the kid, as his or her game seems to generate the joy or misery that Dad and Mom feels. Beagling can be like that. People can live vicariously through the dogs, and feel that the dogs' successes are our own. In truth, I am less of a coach and more of a bus driver/cook when it comes to my role in the success of the dogs. Shooting a rabbit is something I do, but it is because the dogs put in the hard work of keeping the chase going until I got a shot. Moreover, if I miss, they keep working until I get another opportunity. There is little difference between me shooting a bunny and a fan cheering for a touchdown. Both are a celebratory response to witnessing greatness. I like rabbit hunting. I really like rabbit hunting with friends. It is just fine if your dogs are better than mine—I may try to buy a puppy from you later. Right now, it is September and the preseason is almost over. I am ready for the season, and I hope to have an away game in your neck of the woods, where we can be fans of canine professionals.

Rubber Boots

It is no secret that I tend to run dogs early in the morning. Five o'clock in the morning is the typical time that I drop the tailgate in the summer, meaning I am awake by four. I missed two mornings in a row this past summer, due to my wife, Renee, having surgery on her shoulder. She was not permitted to drive home from the outpatient procedure, so I took her there. The dogs were in a complete state of disbelief when I left the house, early in the morning, without them.

I guess I was still thinking about the briars when the surgeon walked into the room to ask Renee what shoulder would receive the surgery. "Are those medical boots?" I asked him, looking at what appeared to be a cheap pair of barn boots on his feet.

"Yeah," he said, "From Tractor Supply."

"There are better rubber boots available than those things," I said, "I wear rubber boots most mornings of the summer."

"These work fine," he said as he walked away.

"Those boots?" I asked my wife.

"What?" she asked.

"I don't know about this guy working on you," I said to Renee.

"Because you don't like his boots?" she squinted at me.

"Exactly!"

"You're crazy."

"I am guessing he makes a decent salary," I pulled on my beard and leaned back in my seat, "So why not have a good boot? Perhaps it is low standards. If that is the guess, what can we say about his skill in the operating room? Maybe he can't afford anything better, what would that imply about a person making his kind of money?"

"Look," Renee sat up straight in the hospital bed and adjusted the backless gown that they make patients wear, "Not everyone needs to buy expensive rubber boots. And you have to stop watching that BBC Sherlock series on Netflix. He is an excellent surgeon."

"Those aren't even the best boots at Tractor Supply, for crying out loud," I said, "And their best boots aren't that good."

"A lot of doctors wear them," a nurse said, obviously hearing me from the hallway on her stroll into the room. "It keeps their feet dry"

"Oh yeah?" I asked.

"Yep. The floors can be wet in an operating room, depending upon how much rinsing they do."

The surgery only took an hour. Now, Renee was certainly tired because she had to be there early. She is not a morning person. The snooze bar is her best friend. I have seen her utilize two alarm clocks on many instances, using both the alarm clock and her cell phone. It took her nearly four hours to awake from the anesthesia. Once home, she continued sleeping for another six hours. Then, it happened.

The house phone rang and the caller I.D. said that it was Renee's cell phone.

"Where are you?" I answered, "I didn't see you leave the house."

"I am upstairs. Can you bring me a puppy?"

"I guess," I said, "Which one?"

"Fang."

I walked into my study where I had Fang and Blitz, 11-week old littermates, crated together. I let them go outside to pee, then carried Fang upstairs.

"Here you go," I put the pup on her pillow.

An hour later the phone rang again. "Can you come get Fang, he doesn't want to cuddle." Then the calls came fast and furious.

"Can you get me a ginger ale?"

"Can you change the ice packs?"

"I want to see Blitz now."

"Do we have any crackers?"

"Would you make some iced tea?

"Is there still a puppy in our bedroom?"

I began to worry after that question. "No," I answered, "Why?

"There's a wet spot on the pillow."

"Was your ice pack there?"

"Oh yeah," she chuckled to herself, "Thanks."

The next morning, she was up early. In part, this was because she had slept a lot. Also, she was in a lot of pain. They had told her to take pain pills, but due to the news surrounding the problems associated with the said medication, she opted not to take it. I had just put on brush pants and was getting ready to load dogs when the house phone rang.

"Hello," I said.

"I will take that pain pill. Why does it hurt so bad?"

"I am guessing because they had to expose your collarbone to remove the bone spur. They skinned you out like a deer. In that one place."

I took off the brush pants and put on khakis, knowing I wasn't going anywhere.

An hour later the next call came. "Do you know where the secret chocolate is?"

"Wow," I said, "Those drugs are potent. You think that there is a secret candy out there that no one knows exists?"

"It does exist."

"Sure thing, honey," I said.

"No. It isn't honey."

"I was calling you honey. Do you want me to go buy chocolate?"

"We have chocolate. Secret chocolate."

"Sure we do," I decided to agree with her.

"Good. Then you know where it is."

"Absolutely not," I said.

"I didn't think so," she sighed and gave me directions to the chocolate. It was in a closet, up high on a shelf, and under an old winter coat.

"Why are you hiding chocolate?"

"I started doing it after the dogs got into Wesley's Halloween candy since chocolate is poisonous to dogs.

Then, as Wes got older, I did it to make sure that I got some chocolate since he would eat it all. I keep it for stress.

"Like now?"

"Yeah," she yelled, "My shoulder hurts, my pillow is wet from ice packs, and I am awake before the sun has come up! But there is usually some stress every day."

That evening I went into our bedroom and started touching her legs after she had me enter for the 8th time in an hour.

"What are you doing?" she asked.

"I know they operated on your shoulder, but they must have cut your legs too. You aren't walking either."

"Go run dogs."

Well, I did. I decided I better figure out how to get in her good graces again. It was a lot warmer in the evening than in the mornings when I typically run rabbits, so the dogs only lasted a couple hours before I picked them up to give water. On the way home, I bought chocolate and more ginger ale. This is because I can't afford diamonds. I walked into the house and there sat Renee, in the kitchen.

"I feel better," she said.

I extended candy and soda pop to her. She smiled, and I poured a glass of ginger ale. We chuckled about secret chocolate. "I am not saying you should use your left arm," I said, "But I think you should walk around." She agreed, and we found out later that some people just take a very long time to get the anesthesia out of their bodies. I immediately went back to running dogs in the morning.

"Can I go to a field trial next weekend?"

"Yep," she said, "I am off those pills. They just gave me enough for a couple days. The incision is healing well, and the original pain that made me get the surgery is gone. I can drive again."

"Have you seen my good rubber boots?" I asked.

"I gave them to my doctor."

"Hah! Good one. Seriously, where are they?"

"Probably at the hospital."